The Japanese Electronics Challenge

The Japanese Electronics Challenge

TECHNOVA

Edited by Mick McLean

St. Martin's Press, New York

All rights reserved. For information, write:
St. Martin's Press, Inc., 175 Fifth Avenue, New York, NY 10010
Printed in Great Britain
First published in the United States of America in 1983

Library of Congress Card Catalog Number: 82-42710
ISBN 0-312-44066-9

Contents

Part II: Microelectronics in everyday life

Foreword

The world economy is now confronted with a difficult situation of low economic growth, unemployment and inflation. However, we are confident that industrial countries have sufficient economic and technological capability to meet with the challenge to overcome the situation and open up a prosperous future for the world. Technological innovation is one of the most important components for achieving this change. Particularly, remarkable development and innovation resulting from rapid advancement of microelectronics are expected to play a major role for this purpose. Furthermore, the application of microelectronics is expected not only to make revolutionary progress in industrial technology, but also to induce tremendous change in our society and everyday life. It is therefore of greatest concern for members of advanced industrial countries, such as Europe and Japan, to understand how this important technology of microelectronics should be developed and best utilized to meet with our industrial and social goals.

TECHNOVA has been organizing seminars with the theme of 'Cooperation in Industrial Development of Japan and Europe' for the past three years. 'Microelectronics' was taken up as the theme of the seminar in 1980 and 1981, in order to explore the present state of art and the perspectives of future development, in a subject which is of great mutual interest and significance for both sides.

We believe that such informal meetings with candid discussions and a frank exchange of views from Japanese and European participants, who have a leading role and responsibilities in their countries, will shed light on the future of industrial society, and clarify the direction of possible collaboration of Europe and Japan in this technology of great mutual interest.

Major papers presented at the two meetings and subsequent discussions make up the contents of this book. We hope that it will convince a wide group of people of the significance and importance of the subject matter, and of possible options for the future.

Keichi Oshima
July 1982

List of abbreviations

CAD	Computer-Aided Design
CNC	Computer Numerical Control (of machine tools and robots)
CP/NET	A microcomputer network operating system produced by Digital Research of California
CRT	Cathode Ray Tube
DP	Data Processing
EAT	Electronic Automatic Transmission (automotive)
FMS	Flexible Manufacturing Systems
HEMT	High Electron Mobility Transistor
IC	Integrated Circuit
LSI	Large Scale Integration
MTBF	Mean Time Between Failures
MIPS	Millions of Instructions per Second
MITI	Ministry of International Trade and Industry (Japan)
MOS	Metal Oxide Silicon (IC technology)
MP/NET	A microcomputer network operating system
NC	Numerical Control
OA	Office Automation
OCR	Optical Character Recognition
OS	Operating System
PPC	Plain Paper Copier
PTT	Post, Telegraph and Telephone (Authority)
RAM	Random Access Memory
ROM	Read Only Memory
UNIX	A 16-bit computer operating system developed by Bell Laboratories
VCR	Video Cassette Recorder
VLP	Video Laser-disc Player
VTR	Video Tape Recorder (see VCR)
WPM	Words per Minute
ZNIX	A version of UNIX (qv) developed by Zilog

General introduction

The recent successful assault by the Japanese on the world-wide electronics market must be seen as the economic success story of the century. This book brings together the views of many of the most distinguished analysts and business men from Europe and Japan on this new force on the world scene: the Japanese electronics challenge.

These papers are not so much concerned with the history of Japan's initiative in capturing a major share of the world's fastest growing industry, but rather with the development of, and future prospects for, technological change within the industry and the impact of such change on the structure of the industry and everyday life in Europe and Japan.

The points of view expressed are, however, as diverse as the backgrounds and affiliations of the contributors. The first section starts with a socio-political overview of the impact of microelectronics on Western society. Reese is pessimistic: he feels that social stability will be threatened by a wave of technical change as massive as that anticipated by many observers. Only by a radical restructuring of society and by the adoption of more transparent and democratic government policies with respect to technology can European nations survive unscathed.

In contrast the next contributor, Ishii, sees a fresh force for individualization, decentralization and democratization inherent in the technology of microelectronics itself. Thus Japanese companies must cooperate with their overseas counterparts to ensure that electronic products are suitable for the market in which they are offered.

This view is reinforced by Rauwenhoff who, from the point of view of a European industrialist, also sees the necessity for cooperation with Japan. Europe could offer strengths in fundamental research, in computer-aided design and software, in telecommunications and in industrial electronics in exchange for Japanese competance in mass production and VLSI circuits. But such cooperation cannot be complete until Japan removes the barriers that prevent European products and companies entering the Japanese market.

Yamamoto gives a succinct overview of the development of the

Japanese industry to date and its excellent future prospects. The following contributor, Guigonis, is full of admiration for the Japanese achievement and contends that Europe will only be able to compete and cooperate on the same level if it abandons a national orientation and evolves a single unified European approach.

Uenohara sees the main stumbling block to future Japanese progress in electronics as the relative lack of Japanese capability in software. This, for Uenohara, is where the Europeans can help; but he does not mention what the Japanese will offer in exchange.

The last contribution in Part I, by Eliasson, returns to the wider concerns of Reese but draws a conclusion that is diametrically opposed to the latter's. A considerable body of evidence from Swedish studies indicates, according to Eliasson, that not only is the radical nature of the impact of microelectronics technology much overestimated, but also that the social and economic changes it engenders are, at least in Sweden, largely beneficial. It is mainly those countries that lag behind in the adoption of new technology that suffer the consequences of high unemployment and social disruption foreseen by pessimistic observers.

Every observer of Japan's industrial scheme cannot fail to notice the central role of the engineer at all levels of management in the Japanese enterprise, in the civil service and in government.

The discussion that concludes Part I offers a fascinating insight into the vast differences between Europe and Japan in relation to the status of, and priority accorded to, engineering. Such fundamental cultural differences may perhaps act as one of the major barriers to future industrial cooperation and it would seem that Europe has much to learn from the example of its prospective oriental partner.

Part II focuses on the impact of microelectronics on everyday life and here Ishii follows on from his previous contribution to speak of Japan's latest effort to combine electronics with its traditional mechanical engineering skills to produce a new industrial specialization: 'mechatronics'. Even small and medium-sized companies in Japan are using mechatronic technology that could reduce labour needs by as much as two orders of magnitude.

Aigrain takes a much more pessimistic, European, view of the prospects for mechatronics. He points to the desperate shortage of designers in Europe, who can appreciate the demands of mechanical engineering, industrial product design and the potential of electronics. Another barrier, according to Aigrain, is the lack of reliable sensors and actuators, which form the links between machines and microcomputers. This should, therefore, be a top priority for government R & D sponsorship in Europe.

Sasaki, in the contribution which follows, again reflects Japanese optimism about sensor and actuator developments. Indeed it is the slow but steady development of such devices in Japan that has made possible recent advances in mechatronics. He goes on to project a gradual convergence of the traditional branches of the electronics industry with integrated circuits as the core technology. This is a theme often aired in the USA and Europe, but given force by Sasaki with his observation that this trend is ideally suited to the structure of the major Japanese electronics companies which are already highly diversified and vertically integrated.

Leinster, a consultant to a major European electronics manufacturer, switches the focus of attention from the unmanned factory of the future to the electronic office. He gives a standard analysis of the enormous scope for improving office productivity through the use of cheap multifunction terminals linked to communications networks. For Leinster office automation promises to usher in a revolution in the nature of office work: a shift away from routine and hierarchical structures towards a more creative and satisfying allocation of work more suited to individual's needs.

Amou reports that the humanized office is already to some extent a reality in Japan. According to him Japan's offices are already organized on a non-hierarchical group basis with decision making based on consensus. The literary basis of the Japanese language and the complexity of its three alternative alphabets coupled with the culturally determined difference in the organization of work means that the nature of future electronic office systems in Japan will differ considerably from their Western counterparts. The particular needs of the Japanese office can be seen to provide an effective measure of trade protection for Japanese manufacturers. Domestic suppliers have captured more than 90 per cent of all sales of microcomputers and other areas of office equipment such as plain paper copiers and facsimile machines are even better placed.

The Japanese copier industry consists of sixteen firms exporting 66 per cent of their output. In the facsimile field, twenty-one companies export 19 per cent of their production and already in personal computers the thirty firms involved have a healthy export ratio of 15 per cent. If the pattern of development of the Japanese copier industry is repeated with word processors and small computers Japan will be assured of a colossal trade surplus in one of the fastest growing markets of the coming decade.

Faced with this enormous threat from the Japanese in the fields of both factory and office automation, Huart, head of semiconductor operations for a European based multinational, makes a plea for greater cooperation between Japanese and European firms.

Many of the earlier contributors from Europe and Japan assume that a major factor that will retard Japan's future progress in electronics and office automation is its chronic shortage of software skills. Tao, the head of a Japanese software house and publishing organization, forecasts, however, that the number of information processing experts in Japan will rise from 118 000 in 1981 to 600 000 by 1985. He also points out that a personal computer craze has hit Japan with the shock of a tidal wave. A recent computer exhibition at a single Tokyo department store attracted 100 000 visitors in six days and a survey of people in a city street showed that 83.3 per cent of the general public already has some knowledge of microcomputers. It is a long step from this widespread popular interest in microcomputers to the establishment of a professional body of software experts, but the fact that many Japanese schoolchildren may well be more familiar with computer languages like Basic than with their own written language bodes well for the future of the Japanese software industry.

The concluding discussion re-explores the topics covered earlier: the relationship between microelectronics and employment, for example, and the chronic problem of Japan's trade surplus. No easy answers emerge; it is clear, however, that some form of cooperation between Europe and Japan in the field of electronics is inevitable. The two TECHNOVA seminars reported in this book have done much to expose the concerns and aspirations of Europeans and Japanese; but it is certain that TECHNOVA's aims are far from accomplished. The contributions presented here represent just the first tentative steps in coming to terms with the Japanese electronics challenge.

Mick McLean

PART I: MICROELECTRONICS AND INDUSTRIAL CHANGE IN JAPAN AND EUROPE

Introduction

LOUIS DE GUIRINGAUD
Former Minister of Foreign Affairs,
France

The greatest problem faced by the European economy, and indeed the whole Western world, at the moment is unemployment. While some of this unemployment is structural and seems to be unavoidable, a number of European countries are now becoming concerned that additional unemployment will add to the structural unemployment. Many believe this 'extra' unemployment is due to the high rate of productivity in Japanese industry, and that it could push the European economies further into recession and possibly into economic jeopardy.

Given the high rate of productivity in Japanese industry, the possibilities and opportunities of microelectronics have not yet been exploited to the full. Once these opportunities have been grasped, one wonders how the present imbalance in trade will affect relations between Europe and Japan. It will also be interesting to see how political relations between the two blocs develop in the future.

There are no obvious, ready-made answers to these questions. The issues raised are manifold, and I shall only mention a few by way of illustration.

The development of the possibilities offered by microelectronics will depend not only on the development of the technology, but also on software. Certainly, Japan occupies a privileged role in the industry with respect to large scale integration technology (LSI). One wonders how Europe and Japan can cooperate in software production?

This raises a second question. Developing applications for microelectronics will reduce the number of jobs on the microelectronics user side and increase the shortage of skilled labour for software manufacturers and users. I believe it is extremely desirable that we should consider how Europe and Japan will react to these conflicting trends.

Then we have a third set of problems. The development of

microprocessors will bring about light, small and middle sized industries, with high technological capabilities, that will specialize in developing application programmes and integrated systems configurations. What will become of these enterprises in Europe and Japan? Comparing prospects can be very useful and can produce much information for those speculating about the future of electronics and of society as a whole.

Microprocessors have been used by the general public in devices such as pocket calculators, washing machines and sewing machines. We will soon see the use of microprocessors spread to public transport, automobiles, office automation, word processing, photocopiers, cash registers and retail distribution equipment. Those of us entrusted with the mission of laying the basis for the future may wonder what the impact of these new products might be in both Japan and Europe. All these questions are important because they have serious social and economic implications. It is a justification of the theme of this book.

We do not pretend to give final or comprehensive answers; instead we simply attempt to prompt further progress in the knowledge and understanding of microelectronics. Quite obviously, there is broad scope for cooperation between Japan and Europe, and areas of possible conflict. The contributors narrow down and define the nature of these areas, and in doing so enable the reader to arrive at a better understanding, not only of the problems raised along the way, but also of the objectives and attitudes held in Japan and Europe. I hope that out of a mutual understanding will blossom cooperation for the welfare of society and the consolidation of peaceful relations between Japan and Europe.

KEICHI OSHIMA
Department of Nuclear Engineering,
University of Tokyo, Japan

Both parts of the world can and should cooperate on this important issues of relations between European and Japanese industry. I think this is the most important element for the future of the world's economy. Specifically, microelectronics is an issue which demands urgent consideration. We would all agree that LSI and VLSI technology is reaching a breakthrough point, but with respect to applications and software, there exists quite a variety of opinions. Some are very pessimistic, and take the view that social disruption and unemployment will result. The other extreme is very optimistic, believing that microelectronics will create a new type of world, the information society, heralding an era of prosperity, diversification and decentralization. I think both viewpoints are valid. The Japanese take the optimistic view, while maybe in Europe there is a little more pessimism. Nobody wants to create conflict or friction among us, thus an opportunity such as this to air the main issues is most timely. Unfortunately, for geographical reasons, we have had to limit our discussions to Japan and Europe.

It is time to consider the issues from both sides, and I hope that we shall have an impact on the policies of companies and governments in developing the future of new technology, especially its application in the software field.

1 The economic and social implications of the applications of microelectronics

Jurgen Reese, University of Kassel,
W. Germany

PRELIMINARY REMARKS

Microprocessors have greatly increased the capacity of data processing. The micro-dimension has placed millions of logical functions on a tiny chip and at a decreasing cost. It enables us to rationalize:

— consumer products (electronic washing machines, calculators, etc.);
— use of scarce raw materials and energy (controlling heating plants, etc.);
— production (robots, etc.);
— information (information systems, computer diagnosis, etc.);
— communication (computer conferencing, satellite TV, etc.);
— administration (office automation).

The many uses of microprocessors makes them a product of considerable economic importance. But the main economic and social impact arises from their applications in socio-technical environments. Thus it makes sense to mention here both microprocessors and their applications.

Many people acknowledge the revolutionary power of microprocessors. They are impressed by the degree of integration of electronic functions. But we must remember that the level of integration cannot always be fully utilized. For example software specialists may say today, 'Technicians offer us a hardware performance improvement factor of 500, but what do we do with it?' Nor are all the possible applications economically viable. For instance the electronically controlled washing machine is on the market at a higher price than the mechanical version. And last, but not least, not all the technical and economic options are socially beneficial, as I hope to show.

SOCIAL AND POLITICAL AWARENESS

The awareness of technological change and its impact on the individual and society depends upon the existence of observable mass phenomena. The most important effect of information technology is where computers and more communication result in increased productivity. It is these effects which the citizen/consumer feels, rather than trends in industrial statistics. This means for the Federal Republic of Germany:

— lost jobs or lower wages—for example between 1970 and 1977 some 28000 people lost their jobs in the office machinery industry;
— daily use of equipment which strains both the eyes and mind; about 150000 terminals are currently in use;
— irritation at unreadable computer terminology—this constantly affects all citizens/consumers;
— worry about the consequences of the centralized storage of personal data. However, a law for the protection of privacy has given some relief. A federal residence registration law will further regulate what data government agencies may keep on file or pass on to others.

Such anxieties and irritants are certainly not a specifically German problem. But because of a rising tide of publicity they have become a major topic of public discussion that few European politicians can ignore.

The alarm at these obvious consequences of the development of information technology for the individual in society is all the more serious when we look into the future. We must realize that the truly great leap into the information society is yet to come, thanks to the remarkable progress of chip technology and the merger of the currently independent 'message' and 'data' technologies. Applications of technology, such as office automation, electronic mail, electronic payment systems, information and documentation systems, cable television, teleconferences, and industrial robots can no longer be understood as tools to be put aside if disliked, as was the case with previous applications of technology. Instead they aim consciously at a reorganization of social processes which no one in modern society is able to avoid; thus for the individual they have a coercive character.

Increasingly journalists, scientists and politicians have directed their attention during the course of this development to the future social implications of information technology. The above-mentioned experiences, especially unemployment due to rationalization, and the problem of protecting privacy, have raised the subject from pure speculation and have gradually made it available for scientific debate. Today, discussion of the impact of microelectronics, which started with a series of seminars at the Institute of the Future, California, in 1974 seems to have become the domain of European researchers.

AN EXPLANATORY MODEL

In collaboration with colleagues from different disciplines, I have tried to review all relevant impact analyses and come to some general conclusions. We drafted a detailed model of the impact context, or effect interdependence, to explain the complex social effects of information technology. Before it is presented here, I should mention that none of us believes information technology itself to be the motivating power of social and economic change. The term 'impact' is misleading if we deduce from it a causal direction.

Causality

Like every technology, information technology itself is ambivalent. It is the manner in which it is applied that determines whether or not it is for the benefit of mankind. Thus our attention has to be directed towards the applications, and also towards the power structure in our societies by which single applications out of the range of possible options are chosen and realized. Both forms of analysis seem acceptable from the point of view of logic, but they are impracticable. There are many applications of information technology, and the power structure of Western democracies is a separate theme in itself. We therefore decided to take a path between these for our analysis. We looked for prevalent trends in our societies and then analysed the reinforcing or mitigating impact of information technology on these trends. Our conclusion is that this technology operates as an amplifier. But what kinds of trends are amplified? We distinguished between the macro and the micro level.

Macrostructure and trends

Our model differentiates between three systems: the economic, social, and political. Each has at its disposal social norms and organizations which secure its continued existence:

— the economic system is characterized as a market economy

regulated by government intervention—its function is to regulate the supply of goods and means of production according to individual and social demands;
- the social system includes the two subsystems, labour and recreation—its function is the creation of a balance between production demands on the one hand and the development and recreational needs of man on the other;
- the function of the political system is the control of the other two systems, and, when occasion arises, of corrective intervention —in so doing the normative principle of a free and social constitutional state favours compensatory social measures, because they interfere least with the functions of the other two systems.

Changes in the economic system also have consequences for the social system; these in turn frequently force intervention by the political system. The systems are in fact linked. In Western democracies social change is generally initiated in the economic system, from where it spreads via the social to the political system.

Microstructure and trends

This analytical structure makes possible a coherent order of individual microeffects due to technological change—including the social consequences caused by rapidly developing information technology.

Economic impacts

In the economic system, the following changes can be observed, apart from government intervention:

- increased business concentration—true for the information technology sector and also for the production of goods and services, because the technical innovations involve high capital expenditure and thus favour branch leaders;
- structural unemployment—the result of several factors acting together: wage intensive production migrates to low wage countries. The rapid growth of the 'telematics' branch has little effect on the Federal Republic in view of the leading market positions of Japan and the USA. Besides, this branch is capital intensive, which means it has only a minimal effect on employment. The accelerated supply of services, thanks to the applications of new technology, are balanced by corresponding possibilities of rationalization;
- impediment of government infrastructure policy in data and message transmission systems—the result of competition on the

part of giant producers on the world market who want to make their customers dependent on them by supplying incompatible systems and components;
— restriction of economic and cultural options—the result of the need of smaller markets, like West Germany, to acquire expensive hardware and even entire application systems from the US or Japan, for reasons of profitability.

Impact on employment

As a result of the expanding market, pressures of competition—both domestic and export—increase constantly for industry and business. Thus, there exists for them no alternative to rationalization. That is, the extensive use of the potential of information technology. In this manner the economic system causes, through increased pressure for more rationalization, an enforced spread of information technology on the employment and thus the social system. Not counting government intervention, the following changes could occur here:

— reduction in individual professional autonomy—the worker's satisfaction with his job is diminished if, through a heightened dependence on technical systems, the content of his work becomes less varied;
— polarization of professional qualifications—automating jobs which then require lower qualifications puts the less qualified at a special disadvantage, particularly when at the same time chances for advancement to the shrinking number of highly qualified jobs tend to decrease;
— in-house power concentration—in-house (or in-plant) information systems, combined with business concentration, lead to further centralization of information and decision-making at the management level.

Impact on leisure

Just as structural changes in the economic system create increased pressure for rationalization in the employment subsystem, the change in working conditions creates exacerbated competition among those who supply the commodity we call labour. This competition manifests itself in increasing pressure to undergo additional education, schooling and retraining which takes up more and more of the individual's free time. Work encroaches into recreation. Also, further changes in recreational habits can result from the use of information technology:

- atrophy of social contacts—increasing availability of information and entertainment, combined with a decreasing need to visit centres of contact (caused by electronic shopping, working at home, etc.) weaken the need for social communication;
- individual passivity—rationalizing social services by means of information technology leads to a decreasing readiness for communal self-help.

The gradual reorganization of recreation and its erosion by changing patterns of work threatens to diminish its value. This is all the more undesirable because changes in working conditions can subject the individual to high psychological stress, with the result that demands for recreation are bound to rise.

Political impact

Functional disorders in the social system require political intervention and thus an expansion of the functions of the system. The need to regulate working life extends further; the demands for assured social security become greater; medical and psychiatric social services grow more comprehensive. Faced with this pressure, the state itself reaches for the rationalizing potential of information technology. As a result we have an increase in the legal and administrative complexity reaching far beyond the 'natural' bounds of bureaucracy. Thus we also get an increase in the social control of the individual, forced to reveal personal details to prove the legitimacy of a claim. The number of citizens who remain able to comprehend the political programmes and decision-making processes of their countries declines, even when immediately affected by them—as in the case of social legislation. At best, consumer/citizen considers the political system to be a technocratic welfare state.

The model outlined here and the scenario of effects that information technology could exercise on society might well after some additional, focused, impact research, prove in parts to require modification or even prove to be false. In the meantime, however, these findings should serve as a working basis for research and policy regarding technology.

POLICIES

Instruments

The classic function of the state consists of contributing to the solution of those social problems which constantly arise from within the social system and its functional disorders. The most favoured means to accomplish this involve legal regulations for the work environment and compensatory measures within the framework of social policy. In the background, there remains the principle of non-interference in the economic system whose structure must be considered largely responsible for the disordered functions of the social system.

This non-interference is obviously no longer tenable in modern society. Governmental monetary/fiscal and infrastructure policies have become indispensable ingredients of the economic system. In Japan, as in the USA and Europe, there exists a third factor in the form of technology policy, which at first glance appears to combine the advantages of the other two mechanisms. This technology policy shares with infrastructure policy the aim of modernizing the national economy, and also shares with monetary and fiscal policy the universal effect of securing working and living standards for the entire population.

At second glance, however, some problems relating to this technology policy become apparent: contrary to monetary and fiscal policy, it neither directly stimulates economic activity nor does this policy contribute to stabilizing given structures, behaviours, or state affairs; rather it advances technical and social change and in so doing dispenses a large measure of instability and insecurity in the shaping of human life. Contrary to infrastructure policy, the effects of technology policy are not predictable or controllable in advance, as in the case of a motorway or industrial estate. Instead the effects of this policy camouflage themselves for the outside observer as compulsions resulting from the economic system. For that reason the promotion of technology is from a democratic point of view full of problems unless care is taken to make its impact on the social system transparent and thus amenable to democratic controls. This is one of the principal tasks of impact research and policy evaluation.

International framework

Unfortunately national governments face very strong restrictions on their economic policies today. In brief, there is first the importance of information technology in the military equipment field. Most of the money spent on basic innovations in the USA comes from the Pentagon budget. Once created for military purposes, new technologies and their applications are pushed on to the commercial market. As a result the information technology market is, unlike most, a pure seller's market.

Second, the leaders of all industrialized countries have experienced an increasing dependence on oil-producing countries since the first oil crisis in 1973. Energy imports and income transfers to oil countries severely affect a nation's balance of payments. As the national surplus declines or turns into growing deficits, the role of exports between industrialized countries becomes even more important than in the past. Thus the admirable technical achievements and export offensive of a country like Japan appears rational.

On the other hand, the countries of Europe are compelled by international competition to submit to an extreme acceleration of technical and economic change. Compared to the USA and Japan, this change affects the very complex structure of social policy provision in Europe. National consensus, and that means political stability, is based on this complex structure of laws and organizations. Thus social stability will be seriously threatened by this strategy of radical innovation, if Europe does not, within the time available, adapt its internal structures to the use and impact of new information technology applications.

2 Microelectronics and technical innovation in Japanese industry
Takemochi Ishii, Faculty of Engineering,
University of Tokyo, Japan

CHARACTERISTICS OF LARGE SCALE INTEGRATION (LSI)

Semiconductors, computers and particularly large scale integrated circuits (LSIs) have an important influence on a wide range of technologies.

Before 1970, integrated circuits (ICs) were commercially produced with some medium level of integration, but products at this level of integration could not develop new or expanded markets. For instance, desk top calculators had only the capacity which their name implies. In the first half of the 1970s, however, this type of calculator shrank to pocket size as LSI developed. As a result, anyone could afford to buy one, and demand grew rapidly. Large scale integrated circuits could be mass produced so the production cost per unit fell, while quality rose dramatically. The competitive development of calculators eventually gave rise to the microcomputer.

The use of LSI in calculators is known as 'special purpose', whereas in microcomputers it is called 'general purpose'. Programmes are changed to suit the application. In other words, the microcomputer can effectively be applied to a wide range of products or to small production runs by mass producing the hardware and introducing flexibility through software.

The important difference with LSI technology is that it can be used by people who are not experts in electronic engineering, and even by amateurs. Also it is highly stable and reliable. Thus this trend will continue and accelerate. A typical example which demonstrates this stability is the automobile-based microcomputer that operates for a long time without maintenance and which can be operated in a 'hostile' environment. The microcomputer can operate in many environments, such as laboratories, factories, or production sites without excessive maintenance. As the range of applications increases and the durability under severe conditions improves, applications of microcomputers increase in both quality and quantity.

The point of the facts mentioned above is that increased integration from IC to LSI broke through a critical barrier. In other words:

— with miniaturization the calculator attained a human scale, i.e. it could be pocket sized;
— unbelievably low cost could result from mass production, in response to the change in the type of owner (everybody began to own a calculator;
— the general purpose microcomputer could replace the conventional computer;
— the stability and reliability were such that non-experts could become users. The current landslide introduction of LSI in every sector of industry means the breakthrough level has been reached.

LSI AND MACHINES

Japanese industries try to maintain their vitality by strong competition and technological innovation. Once a certain level of LSI is reached, industry seeks to apply it. Each industry tries to use LSI as early as possible and in the most appropriate way in its products, regarding this as the best way to beat the competition.

In particular industries, unrelated to electronics, the initial reaction to LSI was a mixture of confusion, uncertainty, and hope. For example some makers of desk top calculators began to produce digital watches with the result that the makers of conventional watches had to protect their markets by also introducing LSI technology. The desk top calculator can incorporate a clock function and open up new markets by reducing its size to that of a credit card. Further introduction of LSI into everyday life through domestic appliances such as sewing machines has become a race against time.

The biggest impact on society will be through automobiles. Needless to say the automobile itself is the result of fine mechanical engineering and mass production. However, there are electronic components in the automobile's air conditioning, stereo, lighting, and electric motors. When the IC was developed, it was expected that electronics would be used extensively in cars. But this was an illusion. The reason for this is that the IC could not break through the barrier mentioned earlier. Purely mechanical technology could match the IC's capabilities and could sometimes solve a problem more easily. The current level of LSI technology, however, has complex logic circuits and a large memory capacity, and mechanical technology could never match this capability. Anti-skid mechanisms, electronic fuel injection (EFI), cruise computers and electronic automatic transmission (EAT), electronic locks, and microcomputer-controlled seat adjustment will soon become commonplace.

The time has now come when the true impact of the introduction of LSI is being felt. The situation until now has been just a rehearsal. Since the automobile industry is both the most competitive and the largest in the scale of assembly, LSI will suit both the automobile and the electronics industries well. It will be an indispensable part of modern automobile technology by reducing fuel consumption and increasing safety.

Large scale integration will have an irreversible impact on all kinds of machinery—not just on automobiles. It will create a new era in the history of technology—a 'new machine'. This new machine will have highly advanced, computer-like parts, as opposed to the 'old machine' which is mainly composed of structural materials and primitive control systems. For example, conventional machine tools are beginning to be replaced with the numerical control (NC) variety, and the trend is to replace them with computerized numerical control (CNC) systems. Computer aided design (CAD) and flexible manufacturing systems (FMS) are being developed as we move towards the 'new machine'. The effect of LSI is both direct and decisive in this area.

ROBOTS AND THEIR PERIPHERALS

A good example of the 'new machine' is the industrial robot. At its current level of development, the robot is not yet fully equipped with sensors giving it vision or hearing or ways of recognizing figures or language, so it mainly does routine work which does not require a response to changing conditions. More advanced robots have, however, been tested experimentally. Even here, LSI and microprocessors are playing an important role; LSI comprises the nervous system of the latest robots.

It is unnecessary to emphasize again the importance of LSI to information processing and communications. Large scale integration acts to some extent as the 'nervous system' of society. Super-computers cannot be made without LSI. The parts which correspond to the sensors of a robot are the man/machine interfaces, the so-called information input channels of information processing or communication systems. Visual images, figures, or sounds could well be used to input information, but it must be coded, preferably in binary code. However, LSI is removing this constraint—for instance voice input was impossible ten years ago, but is now becoming possible.

Pattern recognition of figures is being improved by microcomputers, and output as well as input by these means is also possible. Image processing, for example, Kanji ideograms, is becoming increasingly important for the Japanese. This kind of processing will soon be used in Japan: the input and output of data using Kanji will be possible by the mid-eighties, a long way behind countries which use the Roman alphabet. When this function is added to information processing machines the impact will be immeasurable.

Large scale integration technology can not only make sound output from computers cheap; it also makes the pre-packed 'sound package' possible, using a Read Only Memory (ROM). This has just begun, but will become more common as LSI develops. For example, voice communication while driving and translation and language exercises will soon be available. There are already established applications in entertainment, such as the generation of pictures for TV games solely by means of LSI circuitry.

INFORMATION DISTRIBUTION AND DECENTRALIZATION

Large scale integration will affect technology as a whole and induce changes in the structure of industry. It will also affect urban and national development planning. It can also play an important part in changing the 'structural principle' of the whole of society through decentralization.

An example is the 'new machine' mentioned in the preceding section which is capable of self-replication. This has already happened in some of the most advanced companies: the production of robots by robots. More research and development will bring about this era of the 'new machine'—a new experience for the human race. The principle of this age will be similar to the behaviour of deoxyribonucleic acid (DNA).

The duplication and self-multiplication characteristics of DNA are just like the production of LSI chips, or the printing of books: they are all basically the duplication and propagation of information. Almost ten years have passed since theories of the 'information society' were first advanced. The essence of the change in the structure of industrial society is contained in this concept of the 'information society', including the rationalization of industry, the integration of knowledge and the application of highly advanced technology to industry. Until the invention of LSI, however, this was no more than a concept as the hardware did not exist. Today LSI could be the decisive force in changing the industrialized society into the information society.

Let us now consider the relationship between LSI and the trend towards decentralization. Decentralized systems will be installed in industrial plants using LSI and microcomputers. Only centralized systems were previously possible without LSI. The 'new machine' and the information society will be characterized by decentralization and the benefits will far outweigh those of scale.

What are the benefits of decentralization? The answer is the variety and flexibility of each component: each part of a system will have its own unique characteristic. The aim of decentralization is to bring out their potential. The benefits of centralization are only possible by using factors common to all sectors of the system: elements not common to the system are left out, and variety becomes like a buried resource.

The break away from uniformity is symbolic of the change in industrial structure and the application of advanced technology: the stress is laid on variety. In the industrial society, uniform mass production is the result of mass production technology. Large scale integration is changing industrialized society into the information society with the emphasis on decentralization and variety.

Although the concept of centralization and decentralization contradict each other, centralization, which can integrate common parts of a system, and decentralization, which introduces variety, must coexist. This is the most realistic approach for the Japanese at least.

ACCEPTANCE OF MICROCOMPUTERS BY JAPANESE INDUSTRY

The decentralization mentioned above is characterized by variety; or to put it another way, by a respect for individuality. Look at the example of the wrist watch. The daily life of a whole town used to be controlled by the church clock. As families could afford to buy their own clocks, they could manage their own lives. When people had their own wrist watches, they could organize their own time. However, an increase in the number of wrist watches meant that the church clock was needed only to set the time. The widespread propagation of LSI is like the point at which people began to own their own wrist watches.

In the Japanese employment system, a company's main concern is how to get the best from each employee. The use of LSI can promote decentralization, respect variety and enhance the capability of each employee. Japanese firms try to introduce employees' originality into computer programs and take note of their individuality; decentralization and informatization are adapted, and in Japan, at least, the new machine era will begin at the instigation of private companies.

This does not mean that private companies will take part in an unfair trade war against overseas firms. International cooperation in technology will be indispensable in the era of the new machine. By expanding the product market through variety and internationalization, software becomes more important than hardware, compared to the products of the old machine era—the products of the uniform industrial society. This has already happened in the computer industry. Sophistication of products goes hand-in-hand with the growing importance of software. However, software is highly dependent on the customs and culture of a country—its language, for example. Therefore good software cannot be written without international cooperation between engineers. This is why Japanese firms encourage the use of micro computer in-house and also encourage international cooperation on technology. International cooperation will be the decisive element in competition. Good technological partners should be able to exchange good software. This should be carried out on the basis of national cooperation, so that it may develop into peaceful coexistence and mutual prosperity.

3 Microelectronics: A challenge to industry

Ferdinand Rauwenhoff, Senior Managing Director,
Electronic Components and Materials Division,
NV Philips, Holland

It is intended here to treat microelectronics as a specific case to illustrate the broader issues of a general industrial nature, and also the cooperation between Japan and Europe. For that purpose I would like to analyse briefly the present economic position and some relevant issues relating to Japan and Europe in the industrial field.

If we look back at the development of the world economy in the fifties and sixties, we see that economic growth was achieved in almost all industrialized countries in the world, both in the Western world and in the socialist bloc, under very diverse political systems. Yet the economic policies pursued in that period all produced comparable results.

It can be said that particularly in Europe industrial maturity and affluence have had a profound effect on economic circumstances. The rising standard of living has changed the attitude of people towards work. It is understandable that industrially mature countries have experienced this phenomenon first, but it is still a matter for conjecture whether all countries that are going through their own industrial revolution will eventually be faced with the consequences of people's desire to work less and to work less hard.

This development has led to a first redistribution of labour: people from Southern Europe and North Africa have moved into the northern European industrialized countries. This movement started when there was a labour shortage, but today it is primarily because of a reduced willingness of the local population to do the tedious and repetitive work in industry, which until now has been unavoidable. In some cases where the cost of labour in European countries has become prohibitive, the work has been moved to Far Eastern countries. This is now happening to Japanese companies that are shifting industrial activities to other Far Eastern countries for cost reasons.

At this stage it might be interesting to compare present-day working conditions in Europe with those in Japan.

Wages: Japanese wage levels are steadily approaching those in Europe, but European wages are still generally higher.

Hours worked: The number of hours worked per year is still on average much higher in Japan than in Europe.

Tax burden: The burden of the collective sector (government expenditure and social security) on the community as a percentage of GNP is very significantly different. In Japan the burden of the collective sector is 24.3 per cent, whereas in Europe it varies between 40 per cent and 60 per cent.

Willingness to work: In Japan it is still very pronounced—in Europe much less so.

Absenteeism: In Japan low, in Europe considerable.

In an open and free world economy it is clear that these differences put European industry at a competitive disadvantage *vis-à-vis* Japan. Although Europe can, and of course should, do her utmost to provide better motivation to work and prevent abuses of social security, this will not correct the total picture.

This has resulted in a trade deficit of the European community with Japan of 3.7×10^9 in the first half of 1980, which is 2.5×10^9 more than the deficit of the first half of 1979. Unless corrective action is taken, this situation will inevitably lead to limitations on imports, the erection of trade barriers and thereby the fragmentation of the economy of the free world into trading blocks. This would seriously jeopardize further economic development in the free world.

What one should always try to do is to correct such situations not by negative measures but by positive ones, and for that purpose one should start by looking at the differences between Europe and Japan.

1 *Public transport systems*: Europe started its highway system just before the Second World War and now has a wide network covering the continent. Japan has only just embarked on this.

2 *Homes and living conditions*: Total living space in Europe per family is larger than in Japan. These two points together mean that there is a tremendous unfilled market in Japan which may lead to interesting new markets in the future, both for Japanese and foreign firms.

3 *Social security and government spending*: These are at higher levels in Europe than they are in Japan.

The result of these and other differences is that the total burden of the collective sector on the economy in Japan is 24 per cent of GNP, as against 40 per cent to 60 per cent in European countries. This amounts to saying that Japan is in a position to create a lot of capital that is available for financing industry. Therefore reductions in public spending in Europe seem to be advisable as one way to reduce the imbalance.

An open and free world economy is essential for the continued growth and prosperity of the western world. Differences between Europe and Japan are evident here also. Although officially the two markets are open to each other, the situation is different in practice. The Japanese market is in fact closed for European participation, especially for those industries considered to have a dynamic future. Notable examples are the video cassette recorder (VCR) and video long play (VLP).

This closed character of the Japanese market is very often not the result of formal trade barriers, but of the system of captive distributors. In addition there is the government's enforcement of Japanese standards, and the government's policy of preventing foreign companies acquiring majority interests in Japanese firms.

These differences between the economic and social systems of Europe and Japan indicate the direction in which solutions for better cooperation can be found, but I would now like to deal with a more specific issue in the industrial field where Europe could improve and secure a continued free trade relationship with Japan, because both parties could take advantage of each other's weak and strong points.

Basically, European R&D is very strong, but not sufficiently exploited. Japan's successes in the manufacture of cameras, automobiles, and microelectronics did not depend on originality and leadership in R&D, but on the ability of Japanese industry to manufacture existing products efficiently, and to improve upon them.

The following examples serve to illustrate this:

1 the single lens reflex camera, the basis of the Japanese camera industry, was first made in Germany in 1936;
2 Japanese automobiles have only slowly been introducing features that European cars already incorporate, such as front wheel drive, independent suspension and radial tyres;
3 European TV set makers were already introducing integrated circuits in TV sets when Japanese companies (stimulated by supportive tax measures) were replacing valves with transistors;
4 many Japanese patents are additions to or improvements on existing ideas, rather than real innovations—although of course exceptions do exist.

Now that Japanese industry has caught up with the USA and

Europe, and in certain cases surpassed them, it has arrived at a point where it is vital to accelerate real research. Japan is very much aware of this, but the fact remains that European innovative research is still very strong, and Europeans should be able to turn this to advantage. This is explained by a further analysis of the microelectronics industry.

Japanese industry has concentrated mainly on *one* sector—the digital sector, and on *one* technology—MOS (metal oxide silicon). Memories were the first products introduced, followed by microprocessors. The aim was clearly the total computer market, first at the high end and then moving down to the low end, with the proliferation of digital devices used in everyday life, such as clocks, wristwatches, calculators, office equipment, and so on.

It seems improbable that European industry will ever be able to compete with the Japanese in cost and quality for products like dynamic RAMs (random access memories), wristwatches, and calculators. Although none of these products was originally invented in Japan, they have been so well manufactured that, bearing in mind the adverse competitive position already mentioned, Europe should not even try to catch up.

But in new microprocessors, other forms of logic and particularly CAD (computer aided design), and software, Europe still has a good chance. Software in our digital world is rapidly becoming much more expensive than hardware. Software development requires brains, not factories. It could be an excellent European export product. Moreover Japan is not a leading producer of software or CAD (at least not yet).

In the digital products market, other rewarding areas requiring microelectronics are apparent, namely telecommunications and industrial products. Bipolar, analogue and digital products, not the main areas of specialization of the Japanese today, will play a leading role in these areas, in which performance is often of greater importance than cost considerations. If the Europeans promote their own special strengths in these areas, they stand a good chance of breaking into the Japanese market and reducing the trade deficit.

A condition of this is, of course, that the market becomes a genuinely open one, and that Japan recognizes the necessity to be more open to European products, including new products with a future, in order to continue her own export efforts in Europe. In all fairness, we Europeans only ask for reciprocity. In this way the two partners in trade, Japan and Europe, could each develop in the field in which it has a comparative advantage. Trade would then result in specialization and cheaper production for both. It should become as easy for European manufacturers to establish or acquire factories in Japan, so that they can cater directly to the Japanese customer and adjust product specifications to local tastes and requirements, as it is today for a Japanese industry to settle down in Europe.

If this could be achieved, then continued cooperation and trade between Japan and Europe would be guaranteed. This would contribute a great deal to the stability and future development of society.

4 Microelectronics and society

Takuma Yamamoto, Managing Director,
Fujitsu Ltd., Japan

Microelectronics encompasses the entire body of the electronics art which is connected with, or applied to, the realization of electronics circuits, systems or subsystems from extremely small parts or devices.

This definition was given in 1962 by Dr Keonjian in his book entitled *Microelectronics*. What has been accomplished in the seventeen-year history of microelectronics can be traced through the progress of semiconductor technologies, and especially by LSI and its related arts. Two prime examples are IC memory, which has contributed greatly to the rapid development of large computers, and the micro-computer, which has made it possible to produce goods which have greatly influenced people's daily lives.

Here we shall concentrate on IC memory and microcomputers to show the effectiveness of microelectronics in finished products. The advantages of microelectronics are: reduced costs, improved reliability, and miniaturization.

The progress and influence of LSI technology is illustrated in the accompanying figures. Figure 1 shows the trend in the price of microchips, as a function of price per bit on a 4–6 mm^2 chip. In four years the price of memory declines by a factor of about ten. In industry this is a revolution rather than a reformation. Integration is easier to achieve in memory rather than logic circuits because of their comparatively simple structure. As a result the magnetic core memory in use for main memory in computers a few years ago has now been replaced by IC memory. Memory costs have dropped dramatically, and this should continue at an even greater rate, helped of course by the greater demand for computers.

As computers get larger, more and more IC memories are used, and it becomes important to develop better methods of heat dissipation and interchip wiring.

The drop in memory costs also affects microcomputers (see Figure 2), and the effect is especially important in Japan, where most of the computer manufacturers also develop, produce and sell ICs.

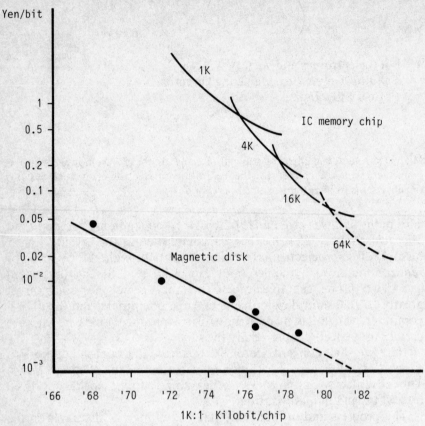

Figure 1   Change in IC memory chip price.

THE SOCIAL IMPACT OF THE MICROCOMPUTER

The popularity of the general-purpose computer has led to an increased demand for software, to such a degree that some people fear that there will be a shortage of specialists to deal with applications technology by around 1985. For example, the Toyota motor company used not to recruit graduates in electrical engineering, electronics, or data processing, but now they are starting to recruit more, which has led to a shortage of such graduates for the computer industry. Thus changes in industry are being reflected by changes in the educational system.

Figure 3 (a well-known figure) shows the ratio of software to hardware costs as a function of time. By 1985, hardware will account for less than 20 per cent of the cost of a computer installation,

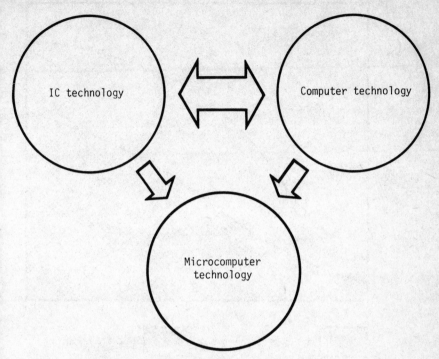

Figure 2   Transition and influence between various technologies.

and most of the cost will be for software and mainly the main-tenance of software. But what is the ratio for microcomputers?

Figure 4 shows the result of a study made in Japan. Respondents to a questionnaire mostly agreed that the relative cost of software for microcomputers is very much less than for general-purpose computers. This is not surprising, considering the position the micro-computer already holds in society, as shown in Figure 5. Figure 5 illustrates the way computers are distributed, with small numbers of the very largest machines and large numbers of micros.

The characteristics of growth in technological terms of large computers and microcomputers is shown in Figure 6. The difference is easy to see: microcomputers and microprocessors tend to develop in a straight line manner, whereas large computer models do not change every year, which leads to a stepwise rate of increase.

The linear growth rate of the power of microcomputers has a direct effect on the ease of economic exploitation of these devices. The result is that microcomputers will make their way into society more quickly in the following applications:

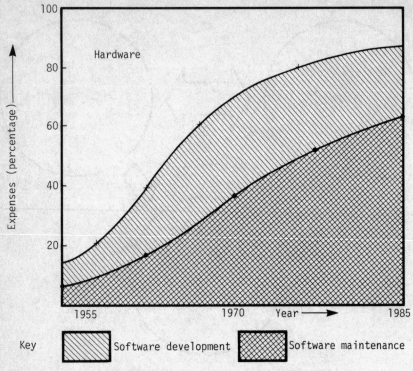

Figure 3   Trends in cost of hardware and software. *Source*: B. W. Boehm.

— numerical calculation (electronic calculators, etc.);
— control of machinery (microwave ovens, automobile engines);
— voice synthesis;
— voice recognition;
— natural language processing.

It is evident that microcomputer-based products have become extremely popular in Japan over the last few years. The following facts illustrate this:

1 The value of ICs sold between 1974 and 1979 by eight Japanese IC manufacturers, as shown in Figure 7, together with a forecast for 1980.

2 The increase in microcomputer-based products shipped over the same period is shown in Figure 8. These products are roughly classified thus:

(a) electrical household appliances (microwave ovens, air conditioners, washing machines, refrigerators, kerosene heaters, etc.);

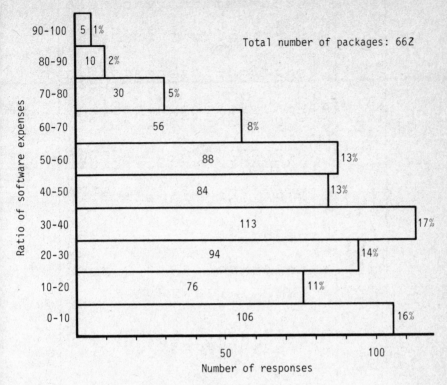

Figure 4   Cost ratio for software to total microcomputer price.

(b) colour television sets, video tape recorders;

(c) stereo and other audio equipment (amplifiers, tuners, record players, stereo sets, radios, car stereos, CB transceivers, tape decks/cassette tape decks);

(d) office machines (accounting machines, indirect-type electro-static copying machines, typewriters, electronic cash registers, facsimile machines);

(e) computer peripherals and terminals;

(f) other fields such as NC machine tools and automatic vending machines.

3 Table 1 shows the rate at which microcomputers are being adopted in Japan for the above categories, except (e) and (f) which belong to higher level microcomputer applications. The numbers in brackets show the percentage of products using microcomputers. Looking at microwave ovens, we see a rapid rate of growth from 25 per cent in 1978 to 40 per cent in 1982.

Table 1   State and trend of microcomputer popularization in Japan

	OUTPUT: thousand units/year				Number of microcomputer-applied units: thousand units/year (coefficient of utilization)			
	1978	1979	1980	(1982)	1978	1979	1980	(1982)
Microwave ovens	1857	1767	1577	1615	464 (25)	530 (25)	639 (40)	888 (55)
Fast food heaters	1577	1618	1070	1655	15 (1)	48 (3)	53 (5)	200 (12)
Air conditioners	3864	5478	5100	5560	190 (5)	820 (15)	1275 (25)	1945 (35)
Refrigerators	4675	4989	5050	5190	95 (2)	250 (5)	350 (7)	520 (10)
Washing machines	4723	4351	4400	4445	21 (0.5)	44 (1)	110 (2.5)	310 (7)
Colour TV sets	8937	9485	9652	9831	536 (6)	1043 (11)	1834 (19)	2753 (28)
Video tape recorders	1559	2245	2837	4131	234 (15)	920 (41)	1560 (55)	3016 (73)
Car stereos	11140	10500	11140	11700	–	320 (3)	530 (5)	1170 (10)
Stereo sets	3140	2940	2820	2820	–	60 (2)	140 (5)	280 (10)
Amplifiers	6840	5590	6160	7180	50 (2)	110 (2)	310 (5)	720 (10)
Tuners	2680	2820	2950	3220	190 (3)	140 (5)	200 (8)	550 (17)
Record players	6410	5570	5770	6090	190 (3)	280 (5)	580 (10)	910 (15)
Transceivers	1310	740	390	390	–	–	20 (5)	40 (10)
Tape decks	27800	28400	30600	33400	1400 (5)	2800 (10)	6100 (20)	8400 (25)
Ordinary radios	7000	3970	3500	4200	80 (1)	200 (5)	350 (10)	840 (20)
Car radios	8370	9210	10050	10880	–	460 (5)	500 (5)	1090 (10)
Accounting machines	14.6	18	21.1	25.4	5.8 (40)	14.4 (80)	19.0 (90)	24.1 (95)
Copying machines (PPC)	560	767	850	1265	84 (15)	307 (40)	595 (70)	1012 (80)
Typewriters	1813	1771	1723	1904	181 (10)	354 (20)	517 (30)	762 (40)
Electronic cash registers	745	1024	1009	1121	596 (80)	922 (90)	959 (95)	1065 (95)
Facsimile	35	55	78	114	17.6 (50)	38.2 (70)	70 (70)	108 (95)

[Research by Japan Electronic Industry Promotion Association in March 1980.]
Note: NC machinery and computer peripherals are not listed in this table.

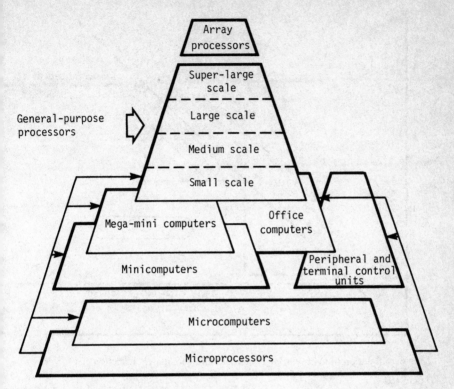

Figure 5   Distribution of computers.

4 Figure 9 is a typical example—the video tape recorder. In the graph on the right, showing the decline in price of VTRs, the increase in price in 1980 is because of the plan to upgrade the microcomputer used.

THE FUTURE OF MICROELECTRONICS

Automotive electronics. The areas in which electronics can contribute most to improving automobile performance are:

(a) emission control (engine control);
(b) fuel economy (engine control);
(c) entertainment (trip computers, composite sound services);
(d) safety (anti-skid control, etc.);
(e) driveability.

In September 1978, General Motors announced that a 10–15 per

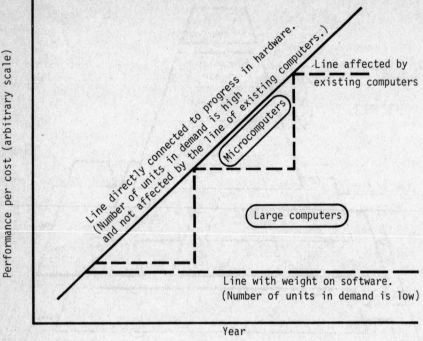

Figure 6   Relationship between large scale and microcomputer characteristics.

cent fuel saving could theoretically be realized if the engine were controlled by microcomputer. Toyota and Nissan of Japan have now also announced new models with microcomputer engine control, and are claiming fuel savings of 10 per cent. It is questionable in both cases whether the whole saving results from the computer control element, but in any case the trend is welcome.

The subjects (a)–(d) above are logical applications of the microcomputer, and are not necessarily very exciting. Automotive electronics has progressed fairly evenly except in the area of making the actual task of driving easier—this remains a topic for the future. For example, it would be desirable to have a car with acceleration characteristics tailored to whoever happened to be driving. Considering the rate at which microcomputers are now advancing in the fields of character and voice recognition, a personalized acceleration system may not be as far-fetched as it sounds.

The most basic effect of improving various automobile functions through microcomputers is that the automobile becomes more flexible to future changes that may come about due to changing social conditions. For instance, even if gasoline is replaced by some

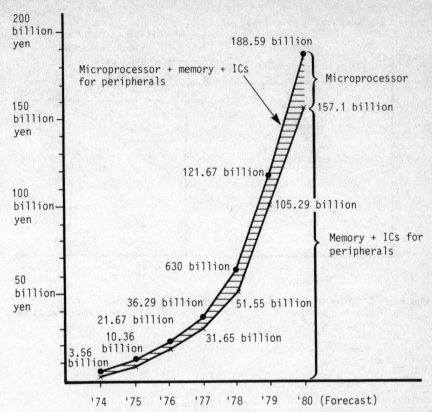

Figure 7   Sales of microprocessors and memory by year. (Eight IC manufacturers in Japan.) (Research by Japan Electronic Industry Promotion Association, March 1980: 55-A-171.)

other fuel in the future, the basic design for engine control units would not have to be altered. An essential feature of computers is that they give us the freedom to pursue diversity, and to select freely the course we wish to take.

Not only in Japan but throughout the whole world we are suffering from the shortage of oil. In order to cope with this energy shortage we must utilize microelectronics as a tool for this purpose and a potent weapon for use in all countries.

Fujitsu recently announced that it is developing a high electron mobility transistor (HEMT), using gallium arsenide rather than silicon. This will be 300 to 1000 times faster than current types. Using it we will be able to build very large 'super computers'. Such super computers will be needed, for example, for the simulation of nuclear reactions, for testing complete aircraft airframes, and for

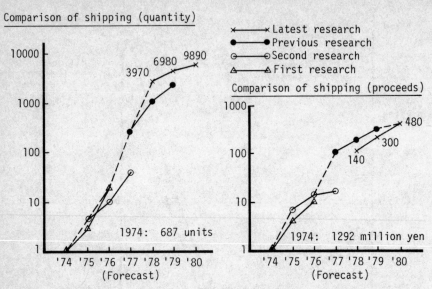

Figure 8   Trends in shipment of microcomputer-applied equipment (compared to 1974 as a base). (Research by Japan Electronic Industry Promotion Association, March 1980: 55–A–171.)

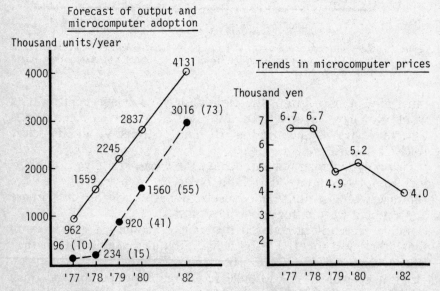

Figure 9   Production state of videotape recorders and microcomputer trends. (Research by Japan Electronic Industry Promotion Association, March 1980: 55–A–171.)

meteorological forecasting on a global scale. In this type of work, physicists have coined the word 'computer physics'. Computer physics is as yet still not equipped to handle large-scale experiments because it takes such a long time to generate curves between the experiment points.

As a tool of science there is a demand for the large computer and it is already being used. For example, a joint study of plasma physics has started between the United States and Japan. It will be necessary to have large computers for this study, and for the Japanese team to have one at least as large as the American one, if not larger.

Land and sea surveys by satellite are another area where super computers will be needed. Table 2 shows, in the first column, the computing requirements to generate a resolution of 80 metres using the Landsat satellite to be launched shortly by the Americans. A resolution of 80 metres can be obtained with a computer of about 3×10^6 instructions per second (MIPS) power, but in three years' time there will be a need on the part of the scientists for a resolution of 30 metres, which will need a computer with a power of about 1000 MIPS.

Table 2 Computer performance necessary for video data processing

	Present	*In 5 years*	*In 10 years*
Resolution	80 m	30 m	10 m
Number of channels	4	7	7
Number of sensors	1	2 ∿ 3	5
Number of images/day	10 (Areas surrounding Japan)	50 ∿ 100 (Far East, Southeast Asia)	200 ∿ 300 (?)
Computer performance	3 MIPS	∿ 1000 MIPS	∿ 50000 MIPS

One of the great advantages of microelectronics is reliability, and a prime example of this is in submarine cables. To give an example of the importance of high reliability, in a submarine cable system on a 3000 km route on most wide band systems more than 500 repeaters spaced at about 6 km intervals will be installed along the ocean floor 8000 metres down. At most, only one or two failures can be tolerated in twenty-five years, which corresponds to a mean time between failures (MTBF) of 5000 years for each submarine repeater. Repeaters of such high reliability can result only when each phase of the production process, from the design of the circuits and parts to the actual production, uses highly reliable design techniques and is subject to extremely rigid quality control. Each transistor, for example, is checked for minute variations in a short-term test to guarantee characteristic variations of under 3 per cent in twenty-five years, using an extremely precise screening set with a temperature setting error of ±0.01°C and variation measuring precision ±0.02 per cent.

Early submarine cables used very robust vacuum tubes connected in parallel, and could be used only for low capacities (several tens of telephone channels). In present systems, however, as a result of progress in microelectronics, transistors have replaced vacuum tubes and the systems carry from several thousand to ten thousand channels. In Japan, a variety of wide band transistor submarine cables have been developed. The biggest systems can transmit colour TV programmes, which require 1000 times the band width of telephone circuits, and 900 channels of telephone signals as well. Fujitsu has developed these systems and laid cables not only in the seas around Japan, but also around South East Asia, areas of Northern Europe (between West Germany and Scandinavia), and the Mediterranean (a domestic cable for Libya, carrying TV). These systems are operating successfully.

At present a 10800 channel system is under field trials. The system uses 1000 repeaters spaced at about 3 km intervals for the 3000 km route. The need for high reliability in the repeaters is obviously very great, so analogue cable systems are reaching their limits, both technologically and economically. We feel that the breakthrough will come with digital optical fibre systems, which are being intensively studied in Japan and elsewhere, in order to make the best use of the unique characteristics of optical fibres, which are low losses, small size and low weight.

Submarine digital systems have not yet been put into practice because of the high number of repeaters resulting from the high losses of coaxial cables, and because of the large number of parts (more than 1000) required for digital repeaters, which downgrades economy and reliability. We now believe that such a system is possible, however, as a result of the rapid progress in microelectronics, optical devices, optical fibres and LSI technology.

The use of low-loss monomode fibres is expected to extend the repeater spacing to about ten times what it is at present: to about 30 to 50 km. In addition, it is no longer merely a dream to be able to put about 1000 discrete components for one digital repeater into a few LSI chips and obtain higher reliability. It is planned to be able to put short and medium haul systems (1000 to 2000 km) into service within a few years, and long haul systems (up to 8000 km) within ten years.

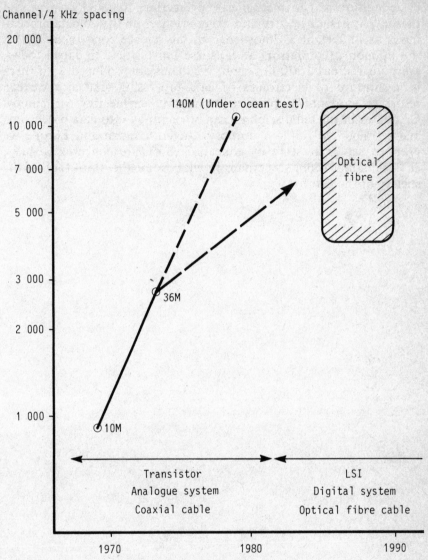

Figure 10 Progress of submarine telecommunication systems in Japan.

One serious problem faced by Japan as well as Western countries is the shortage of data processing graduates. This year, Japanese manufacturers experienced some difficulty when trying to recruit graduates. The question then arose—could the gap be filled by using electrical engineering or information engineering graduates? Data processing is used in all sorts of places: in the chemical industry, in agriculture and in mechanical engineering. It could even be said that in physics, chemistry and other sciences ability in data processing is as important as knowledge of the science concerned. That is the opinion of professors at Japanese universities. In Japan today, every year about 100000 science graduates are produced, so if there is a shortage of electronics or data processing graduates we can resort to students of physics, production engineering, or mining. Graduates in related disciplines can be recruited into data processing, and retrained to suit our purposes. In both Japan and Europe we need to set great store by education. Software concerns language and communication, so perhaps it will become the 'third tool' of the society of the future.

5 Prospects for the development of relations between the European and Japanese microelectronics industries

Edouard Guigonis, Executive Vice President,
Thomson CSF, France

Japanese industry today is in an enviable position in the international microelectronics market. Quantitatively speaking it has gained a significant market share. Qualitatively, Japanese industry has already shown exemplary drive, though it could reinforce its position still further in the coming years.

American competition now finds that it must challenge the Japanese in a few key fields that it had previously dominated. The increase in Japanese activity has made European competitors rather more uncomfortable, since many of them are not so well placed as the Japanese and Americans. It is generally agreed, however, that for the Japanese, this is the just reward of an effective industrial policy. This policy has been quoted as a model of lucidity and coherence in its conception and of continuity and efficiency in its realization. Some of the essential features of this policy merit further attention.

At a very early stage the Japanese became aware of the innovative advantages that could be gained from the advent of semiconductors. As long as fifty years ago, Japan was producing the first solid state detectors, to great general surprise.

As soon as electronics was incorporated into the plan for the reconstruction of the Japanese economy microelectronics took the leading role. Since 1957 a law on the development of electronics laid out the path to be followed, and a longer term plan of action was established. The 1977 VLSI (very large scale integration) project represents just one of the most recent steps taken. One has to admire the mixture of daring and realism at every stage of the process, each successive objective being consolidated and incorporated into a perfectly coherent progression.

The realism appears notably in Japan's systematic recourse to the available USA technology. The daring can be detected in the aim for significant market shares for each product and by the constant ambition to free Japan progressively from its technological dependence. It is the execution of this latter action that particularly holds our attention. Japan has been able to bring into action the nation's skill according to a scheme which combines, in an astonishingly closeknit fashion, state incentives and the vitality of private industry.

The development of microelectronics has been closely associated with the development of equipment and end products. Thus, Japan has benefited from the buoyancy of a high volume internal market to tackle foreign markets on the basis of sufficiently large volume production.

The flexibility of the environment has given rise to some conditions which often appear incompatible to Western eyes. Careful organization of competing industrialists has prevented Japan from exposing itself to accusations of restrictive trade practices. Extensive state financing has been provided without reducing profits: the precarious equilibrium of the balance sheet has been preserved, leading to a compromise involving increasing funds from private financial sources. Public opinion has permitted a constant growth in productivity. Close cooperation between all levels of participants has been an important factor, expressed in constant innovative effort in the area of organizing production. Results obtained in this particular field are concerned with the continuing command of total quality control which reduces direct and indirect costs. All these show that now is the time for Western industrialists to realize the advances the Japanese have made in these fields, and learn a lesson from them.

Faced with this picture, the European situation certainly looks less than rosy. In general, the steps taken to prepare for the advent of microelectronics have so far often been too late, and disjointed in both timing and method. Nor are they sufficiently integrated into an overall development plan for new applications which takes account of the needs of the end user of electronic and information processing equipment.

Since each country has acted independently, one should not be surprised that (to choose one example) on the VLSI programme, the Europeans have, at first glance, spent much more than the Japanese to reach a much less satisfactory overall position.

The industrialists themselves have too often not appreciated the speed and impact that changes in technology would have on their traditional methods. One of the principal attributes of the Japanese is the incredible speed with which they can adapt technical progress to viable commercial realities. The wristwatch industry is a typical case in point. We should beware that it does not happen too often.

But how should the Europeans react? There is one recurring theme in public discussions of the development of trade in microelectronics.

This is the principle of the international division of labour and the evident necessity to apply it to the situation we are facing today.

A few months ago I heard an American industrialist presenting this theory before a European audience. He gave a striking analogy; just as black holes in the universe attract and absorb everything near them, it will be the major poles of the microelectronic industry which will gradually absorb the activities of their neighbours. Just as diodes have given way to transistors, transistors to ICs of small, then medium, then large and very large scale integration, and ICs to microprocessors, so microelectronics is destined to absorb in future the circuits for varying specific applications and then, finally, the end products themselves. Following this analysis and the analogy of the black holes, I would add that we are seeing two galaxies, barely touching (USA and Japan). Each has several black holes. I do not consider that Europe has one single pole of semiconductor activity that could even begin to become a black hole. In fact I ask myself if it is possible that a new pole could even appear today in Europe? What is more to the point, given the level of semiconductor technology, could anyone still have an interest in creating such a pole? This is a brutal diagnosis but I believe that every interested European industrialist should think it over carefully.

There are two important points that stem from this analysis. The first concerns the fundamental idea behind the problem and the other touches on the consequences if Europe was called to give up its efforts.

It is well known that microelectronic competition is dominated by the famous learning curve, according to which, for each product the unit cost of manufacture varies with time according to an inverse function of cumulated volume production. But two flaws can be seen here. First, the late launch of a product makes it difficult to catch up. You just exhaust yourself for nothing: running for a train after it has left the station. Secondly, if two companies start at the same time on the same curve, the one with the larger market share will much more rapidly outstrip his competitor with lower production costs.

It is easy to see that this does not present a very good picture of European industry compared to the hold of USA industry and the ambitions of the Japanese. It is not surprising then that certain disinterested experts advise simply accepting things as they are. In a recent article one of these experts sketched out a possible distribution of roles thus: to the USA, the development of new product; to the Japanese, volume production; to the Europeans the application of software (with the aim, I would add, of meeting only internal demand).

Such a scheme is attractive for two reasons. First it would obviate the need for Europeans to dedicate large amounts of money to R&D and to make other industrial and commercial investments in order to try and keep up with the competition. Second, it highlights the growing importance of software in these fields. It is software, closely linked to the particular market environments which we serve, national and international, which represents the ultimate point of anchorage for our enterprises. And it is this software expertise which provides for the Europeans not only a defence but also an opportunity to strengthen their position. We will then be able to continue to adapt our products to the specific needs of the markets that we serve and master the systems in which these products must become integrated.

To consider that any international distribution of labour could be established by limiting oneself to this ambition of mastering the software of the microelectronic products would be, however, in my opinion a dangerous illusion. Complete mastery of software involves the development of new circuits and is affected by their supply conditions—prices and lead times. These considerations bear such weight that the competition at end product level would be to the detriment of those who do not have any control of software. These companies would be driven back and forced into the simpler activities of final assembly and commercial distribution.

In other fields of industrial activity, international exchanges can accommodate a situation in which a partner will give up one particular sector of activity. It is difficult to see, however, how Europe could cope with giving up in the case of microelectronics. It is not just the direct turnover gained from microelectronics that would be jeopardized. Despite the importance of direct earnings, the primary concern is to maintain the competitiveness of our industries in a technology which has been revealed to be the key to technological evolution for years to come. This is true for many industries, for the electronics industry and for industries on the periphery of electronics.

Considering the energy shortage, where Japan and Europe are in the same difficulties, the position is worsening. But one must bear it in mind if one tries to imagine the possibility of a cooperative relationship between Japanese and European industry in the field of microelectronics. This cooperation is apparently wished for by both parties, yet it is necessary to ensure that the terms of the cooperation are of the same significance for both parties.

In order to try and clarify my theory, I will suggest two very different methods of approaching this problem which both appear to contain serious misapprehensions. The first possibility is that Japanese industrialists will use the ideal of cooperation to disguise their intentions of entering the European market. Frequently, the foremost advantage for the partner is the creation of a number of jobs by setting up a production facility in an economically depressed area. However, this advantage is doubtful, partly because there is a limit to the number of jobs created, and partly because the European partner will be deprived of all capacity for initiative in this crucial area of microelectronics. One can see just how badly such a solution would meet the requirements which I suggested earlier.

On the other hand, it appears to me equally necessary to check a particular approach, European this time, which seeks to establish this desired cooperation on theoretical grounds too distant to be an industrial reality. Here the concern is to show that, in the face of uncontested American dominance, the Japanese and the European will harmonize their united forces to maintain a certain balance.

Moving nearer to the concrete problems which are to be resolved, it seems to me that the reply of a Japanese colleague on this question clearly states the way in which he saw the possibility of cooperation in these fields: 'This collaboration will be difficult to put into practice, either because foreign enterprises will be very competent and thus find it difficult to improve on past performance despite knowledge acquired through the cooperation agreement; or because the foreign company will be incompetent and its cooperation will not be accepted by us.' There we have the problem. Before talking of cooperation, Europeans must establish whether this cooperation will be, in reality, of interest to the Japanese partner, since it supposes that the parties should be on the same level. It is the part of Europeans to establish first their credibility in the eyes of the foreign partner, Japanese or American. Everyone knows how difficult the task will be if it is kept within a national framework and if efforts remain dispersed. It is encouraging, however, to see the emergence of a growing consciousness of the importance of a European plan.

The recent proposals concerning microelectronics introduced by the EEC Commission, although very modest in their ambitions, mark a significant step in the right direction. They underline the fact that the seriousness of the problem is now clearly seen at all political levels in the European countries.

As industrialists we are not willing to encourage any protectionist measures which might hamper the freedom of exchange in international markets. It is up to us to make the necessary effort so that a resort to such measures does not offer itself as the sole possible safeguard.

6 Microelectronics in Japan: Essential resources for industrial growth and social welfare
Michiyuki Uenohara, Managing Director,
Nippon Electric Company Ltd., Japan

The communications industry is considered by some to be fully developed, but in fact it is growing again, due to increasing domestic and international needs, coupled with the introduction of digital technology, stored program control and optical fibre links. The computer is no longer a professional machine confined to a computer centre: it is rapidly penetrating offices, stores, factories and homes. The computer industry has been least affected by the economic slowdown which occurred after the Arab oil embargo of the early 1970s.

Today is the age of computers and communications. The era of their union is about to dawn. This marriage of isolated technologies and markets has been made possible by microelectronics acting as the go-between. This new market will encourage further progress in microelectronics. We can call this concept 'C & C technologies' and 'C & C markets'. These concepts are shown in Figure 1, where the horizontal axis represents communication technology. This technology is changing from an analogue base towards more and more digitalization. The vertical axis represents the move from 'single function' computers to 'multipurpose' and 'distributed processing' computers. The technology is moving and the market system is also changing. Technology and the market are linked by the middle curve, showing the progress through semiconductors to integrated circuits and LSI. This marriage will be fully realized towards the end of this century and should flourish at the beginning of the next.

That modern electronics has made great progress is due largely to advances in solid state device technology. Semiconductor technology is moving rapidly into VLSI. This will drive the microprocessor and the memory to new performance and cost levels. These components will find themselves given to many hitherto unimagined applications in almost all industrial sectors; mechatronics, informatics, etc.

The semiconductor industry is becoming a basic core industry, like the steel and petroleum industries in the past. The progress of

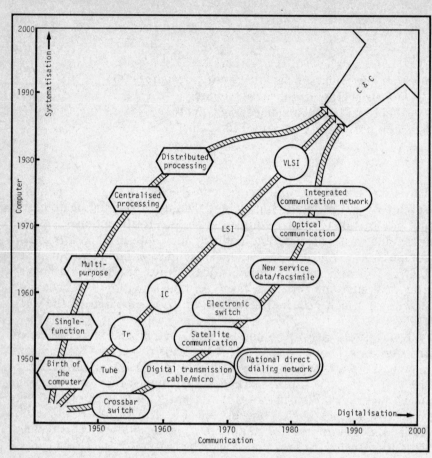

Figure 1   The future of 'C & C'.

the semiconductor industry resembles that of the automobile industry thirty years ago. Future growth is likely to follow the automobile
industry pattern, although we can predict more growth for the semiconductor industry. Hence, the microelectronics revolution and its
implications have become key international issues.

The reasons why the Japanese are putting great effort into the
development of microelectronics are presented in this brief summary
of the trends and potentialities of microelectronics. The most important reason is reflected in the title of my paper: microelectronics
constitute the essential resource for the growth of Japanese industry
and the improvement of Japanese social welfare. I think it is true not
only for Japan but also for the world as a whole.

Microelectronics has characteristics that match most of Japan's fundamental needs. For example, microelectronics saves energy, raw materials, space and manpower, and reduces the cost of products. It is a knowledge-intensive industry that adds high value to products. It adds intelligence to machines and broadens people's work activities. Japan is a small island, much smaller than France and slightly larger than Italy. It has practically no natural resources and insufficient agricultural land to feed more than 100 million people. Since our lives are heavily dependent upon other nations, we have no military power to invade countries with the necessary mineral energy, raw materials and food. Thus we are always in a state of insecurity and Japanese people have to work hard in order to make a living.

We have to import most natural resources and add high value to exports to pay for imports and to support poor nations or our neighbours. No matter how difficult the obstacles and how strong the pressure, we have to cope with them to maintain peaceful co-existence. This is the only way we can survive as we have no military power. We have to cooperate with developing countries to enable them to advance at a faster rate than we do, in order to maintain peace. We have to work harder to meet changes in Japan's industrial structure. The only resource we have is a well educated, diligent people. We have to shift towards a knowledge-intensive and value-added industry, while reducing the consumption of energy and resources.

This, we think, is our responsibility. Microelectronics is the most suitable technology for these objectives. The Japanese Council for Science and Technology, the Industrial Structure Council of the Ministry of International Trade and Industry (MITI), and many other councils and industrial associations reached a consensus on promoting a knowledge-intensive industry in the early 1960s. Electronics was one of these key industries. Based on the Machine and Electronics Industry Promotion Acts, the Large Industrial Technology Research and Development Programme was initiated in 1966. The electronics-oriented projects supported by this programme are listed in Table 1.

All expenses, except for indirect costs, are met by the government. Hence, all key technologies developed have to be open to the public and all patents generated belong to the government. In 1955, the government finance support programme for industrial modernization was amended to cover the development of new computers. In 1968, the key technology research and development of speculative projects was included in the programme. This is an interest-free loan and risk-insured scheme. If the project is successful, the company has to

Table 1   Electronics-oriented large project budget (million yen)

Project	Period	Total budget	1978	1979
Super high performance computer	1966 ∿ 1971	10000	–	–
Pattern information processing system	1971 ∿ 1980	35000	2514	2803
Comprehensive auto-mobile traffic control system	1973 ∿ 1979	7300	585	153
Very high performance laser applied production	1977 ∿ 1983	13000	385	2272
Optical measurement and control system	1979 ∿ 1986	20000	–	51

repay the government. The government finances 50 per cent of direct expenses and the company involved has to finance the rest, including indirect expenses. The 'wired city' project using optical fibre cables, nicknamed HIOVIS, and the VLSI development project are examples of projects financed by this scheme.

The VLSI project started in 1976 and finished at the end of March 1980. The project was basically a cooperative research effort by five computer manufacturers, NEC, Toshiba, Fujitsu, Hitachi and Mitsubishi. The project did not develop final VLSI products, but only the common basic technologies needed for product development by the individual companies. This was necessary for cooperative research to function properly where fiercely competitive free enterprises were involved.

About 100 engineers from the member companies and a government laboratory gathered under one roof, the VLSI Cooperative Research Laboratory, located in NEC's Central Research Laboratory. This was, I think, the first such case in the world. We have gained valuable experience from the project, and this experience may be extended into international cooperation. Now the project is finished, member companies are keenly competing to develop VLSI products—an essential function in free nations.

Microelectronics is a rapidly advancing technology and a key to Japanese industrial development. There are about thirty large electronic companies, 120 medium and many small ones in Japan. Even though they have specialized product lines, they are all aiming at microelectronics in many different ways. Recently other industries, like textiles and chemicals, have promoted microelectronics. Many of them have very similar products. They are competing fiercely and have had to diversify their limited R&D resources. Even so, no one can match the giants in the USA and Europe. In addition, the Japanese professional community has little company-to-company mobility. Engineers stay with one company for their whole careers, and this limits the transfer of technology. Each company has to carry completely overlapping R&D facilities. Such a competitive environment accelerates technological development on the one hand, but reduces the density of individual technologies on the other. This has prompted cooperative R&D and is one reason why Japan has been criticised for merely following European and USA technology, rather than contributing to seed technologies.

Until the early 1960s, Japanese industry received practically no financial support from the government for R&D. That is the scarcely credible truth. Industries in other developed countries had been receiving more than half of their R&D expenditure from government. After the war, which completely destroyed Japanese industry, companies had to work hard to develop their technologies until the early 1960s. To match the advance in world technology and contribute to the advance of science and technology, R&D efforts had to be more effectively coupled and funds for R&D had to be increased. These problems have long been recognized and discussed in all sectors of Japanese society. A reasonable consensus has been reached for practical solutions. We have been practising, in various national projects, some of the tangible results. They are not ideal, but represent particular solutions in the context of the present state of Japanese society.

Japan's economy has been likened to a skyscraper standing on a sandy bed and supported by many steel cables rooted on ground further away. We have been trying to strengthen our foundations by developing our own technologies, maintaining our integrity, and improving our international understanding. We wish to contribute seed technologies for innovations in repayment for the help we have received from America and Europe. Hence, many steel cables that support other nation's skyscrapers may soon be rooted in Japan. We have to work hard to find ways to strengthen international relations for peaceful coexistence.

The future of microelectronics is very bright. It should be a driving power for the revitalization of the world's economy and a tool to enrich society. That is why we are cooperating and working hard to develop microelectronics in Japan. We believe in the future of microelectronics for the betterment of the international community. However, various fears have been voiced concerning the negative aspects of the new technology. One strong criticism is the fear that microelectronics may limit job opportunities and increase unemployment. Another criticism is that it may alter the path of society towards the robotic society widely predicted in science fiction, with far-reaching and destructive effects. Any proposals for change will give rise to anxiety. But we have before us the prospect of advancing society and enriching social welfare by finding new technologies and managing them properly. Similar words of warning have always been uttered in the face of technological innovation, but progress has always expended the labour market and enriched life.

At the beginning of this paper, I mentioned briefly the great opportunity in C & C technology as one form of microelectronics. The idea of C & C is further expanded to include a great and beneficial impact upon society. A feature of this concept is the way in which R&D and application of C & C technology have sought to satisfy human needs, making life fuller and more satisfying. C & C technology must exist for the sake of humanity and must contribute to society. In other words, C & C technology must begin and end with human needs. This concept is extended to 'M & C & C' in a three-dimensional form that means 'huMan society with C & C'. Relations between human society and C & C are shown in Figure 2. To achieve the objectives of M & C & C, we have to develop many key technologies. Four of them are shown in Figure 2, centred on software and system product engineering. Software and system product engineering require huge amounts of manpower from various disciplines, and they create new mass markets. The conventional labour market will provide new opportunities with the aid of microelectronics.

Software production is increasing at a great pace. This profession is still limited to trained professionals, and many are concerned that the imbalance between demand and supply of software workers may limit progress. The development of software production tools using microelectronics will expand this new job area to include many people who have so far been categorized as unsuitable.

New tools and equipment with intelligence will provide 'hands', 'hearing', and 'sight' to the handicapped. International language barriers will be greatly reduced by the development of translation machines. In Japan, preparation of neatly typed documents has been very time-consuming and very costly. However, word processors will soon be able to circulate neatly typed documents at a reasonable cost which will make Japanese business practice more understandable. The complexities of Japanese business communications have been criticized many times in the past.

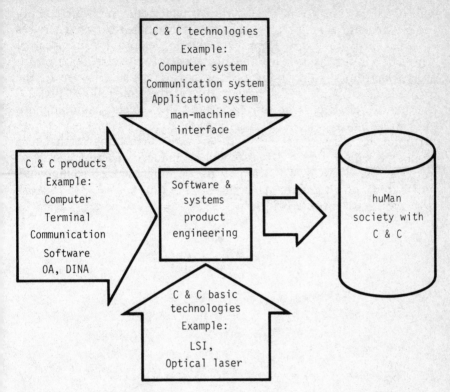

Figure 2   Relationship between society and computers and communication (C&C).

The future of microelectronics is bright; but it is difficult, if not impossible, to provide the human touch. Modern society has been losing the human touch which is imperative for the enrichment of life. In the past, technology has tended to sacrifice the human element to provide more goods and services at a reasonable cost. We now have a chance to reverse this trend through microelectronics. This aim can be achieved only with our sincere efforts. In this respect, there are numerous opportunities to cooperate for the improvement of society, not only in the area of science and technology, but also in the social sciences, in our understanding of the environment, and the development of new 'soft' technologies.

In limited areas of software technology there are enormous opportunities for advance. I often say to NEC software workers: 'Software science technology is not at the stage of science and technology. It is still at the craft stage, the stage of the industrial revolution.' The productivity of software workers is still low. If low productivity continues, no matter how far hardware advances, we will not enjoy the advancement of microelectronic hardware technologies, because a major part of the cost of microelectronic services will be software costs. Then, we will not enjoy the potential of microelectronics because of the high cost of software. As a result, microelectronics will not advance. So hardware and software are the two wheels of work, which have to turn at the same rate. At present, the hardware wheel is turning faster and the vehicle is skidding, not moving in a straight line. This is a cause of concern for us. We have to innovate software science and software engineering so that productivity will increase and costs will be reduced. There are signs of progress, but they are still premature. We Japanese wish to innovate, but I think much greater strength exists in Europe. We wish to work together to solve this great problem.

7 The macroeconomic effects of microelectronics

Gunnar Eliasson, President, Industrial Institute
for Economic and Social Research, Sweden

I believe it was Ludwig Wittgenstein who said that truth depends a lot on how you look at it. This is especially true in the context of microelectronics.

We talk about microelectronics as a revolutionary technology and at the hardware level it is certainly impressive, to say the least. Here we shall examine the effects of this revolution at the aggregate economic level. The important question is just how revolutionary is it at that level? On the one hand, there is the growth potential of this new technology, which has been emphasized by my Japanese colleagues. On the other hand, frightening prospects of mass unemployment have been raised by many and various publications from Europe.

I shall try and elaborate on the studies made into these matters at the Industrial Institute for Economic and Social Research, in Stockholm where I am based. I have a sizeable box of literature at home on the subject. On unemployment prospects, the pessimistic type of literature falls into two categories. In one, the authors tend to emphasize the effects of electronics on the processes of industry alone. They see only that the processes are affected, not the products as well. Furthermore they tend to pick one or two extreme cases and then generalize to the whole of industry. From this they conclude that there will be mass unemployment tomorrow.

The other kind of literature adopts a more theoretical approach. Various model structures are devised, some of which are purely theoretical, some empirical, but all have a certain structure that illustrates what Wittgenstein said. In fact several of these models lead to unemployment however you operate them. I can quote a number of cases where the models lead inevitably, when you examine their structures, to unemployment. My aim is to define the problem in macro terms and try to show the effects on economic structure—particularly on output, costs and unemployment.

The literature tends to agree that, historically speaking, technological improvements are necessary for growth. The graph in Figure 1

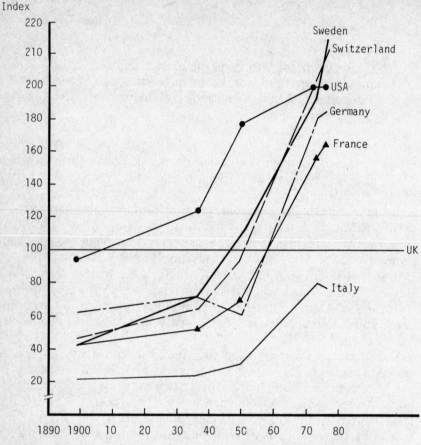

Figure 1   GNP per capita in different countries 1890–1975. (Index: UK = 100.)

shows economic growth, that is the change in GNP over the last eighty-odd years, with the datum of 100 being the GNP of the United Kingdom. You see a tremendous difference in growth rates measured over this considerable period. Sweden and Switzerland have performed quite well, although recently the Swedish authorities have had cause for concern.

The question is: to what extent will microelectronics affect the future projection of growth? Is it a really revolutionary technology when looked at at this level? I doubt it. Anxieties about unemployment are very exaggerated. We cannot find any real substance in the claim that electronics or any other technological change will create unemployment on any scale. But it will create structural change.

As far as production is concerned, our basic conclusion is that electronics enters the production processes, in manufacturing in particular, in a very gradual fashion. It has done so in the past and the case studies and interviews we have done do not suggest any acceleration of the process. And there are other factors that are holding development back and slowing down expansion. So it may be that microelectronics will not generate growth any faster than that experienced in the early 1960s which arose from very different causes. One example of these causes relates to economies of scale, which gave tremendous increases in productivity in the steel sector, which led to considerable structural change in that industry and elsewhere. If you look at this and compare it with what we have learned from our studies of electronics and its applications, it is by no means indisputable that expansion will be faster and more vigorous than in the past.

A point I would like to emphasize is that economists analysing the economy, or even sectors within it, tend to regard the economy as one huge machine in the aggregate. This is quite wrong. If you look at the economy as one big machine, you miss many of the aspects of technical change and its effect on growth. Nevertheless technical change in its various aspects seems to explain a great deal of growth.

We should keep in mind the expression 'structural adjustment', which is a micro-to-macro effect. This is illustrated by the three-way diagram in Figure 2. Thus there are three elements in our study: case studies, a model of the Swedish economy and studies of technical effects at plant level.

The model of the entire Swedish economy is necessary because the study of the effects of electronics on technical change is typical of what economists call a general equilibrium problem, in which all parts of the economy are affected by one change, and the whole model has to settle down to a new equilibrium point before the final effects of the original change can be sorted out.

The complexity of the problem can easily result in misleading conclusions and I believe that this has happened in a number of studies. So we have a micro-macro model that includes a number of real firms in which one can identify technical change in the form of new investments. The model is fed into a computer, and a factor called 'technical change' can be varied to see the effect on the economy as a whole. This factor has been estimated for the twenty-year post-war period. The important thing is that we have measured technical change at plant level.

The next step in our study for the Committee on Electronics and Computers in Industry is to try and reach some sort of conclusion

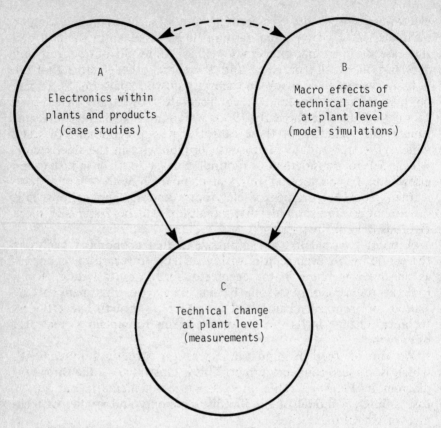

Figure 2   Electronics, technical change and the macroeconomy—the empirical method.

on the effects of technical change on the economy. Referring to Figure 2, once one has established some sort of relationship between A and B, one is able to draw some indirect conclusions about the interaction between A and C, about how electronics may affect the macro side of the economy, especially unemployment, growth, and structural adjustment. One cannot, I believe, approach this problem in a partial study, calculating the effect on labour of one single element in the production process, as one can miss so much. The danger is the tendency to make a big thing out of something that is quite normal and has been going on for years.

Another difficulty is scaling: just because one per cent of electronics is introduced into an application, this does not necessarily mean that a one per cent change occurs in the technical change factor. Technical change in one industry often has a strong effect on unemployment in sectors of other industries. This has happened in

Swedish industry and elsewhere. Structural change in the textile industry over the last thirty years has led to a reduction in the demand for wool, causing sheep farming to decline to one third of its former size, which implies the closure of one medium-sized sheep farm every month for thirty years. That is a sizeable change, a structural change that has been going on ever since the war, and a much larger change than the one we are seeing as a result of the introduction of microelectronics.

The key word behind technical change is structural change, and the fact that the necessary adjustments simply come along as economic forces dictate. This has been going on, especially in the faster growing economies, in the post-war period, but what is happening now in the Swedish economy is that a deliberate policy has been adopted to slow down this change. We have tried to break down the 'residual factor of technical change', that is, to analyse the part of the growth of industrial output not explained by the effect of investment, capital growth, and labour change. This we have done by moving to a macroeconomic model from microeconomic models and from separate studies.

The traditional production function leaves about 75 per cent of growth in industrial output to be explained by this domestic technical factor, in Sweden. In the USA the same measurement produces a figure of about 30 per cent. When we examine the 75 per cent residual at sector level, we find that about 30 per cent of the residual can be explained by structural change, keeping productivity change constant in each sector. We can then break the sector down into company or plant level, and at this level a further 30 per cent of growth is found to be due to structural change between companies in that sector.

At the company level we find that of the residual of 75 per cent of growth in output, half of it is explained by structural change between firms, holding productivity constant within each firm.

Now, going from micro to macro, we have found that perhaps more than 50 per cent of changes in production goals can be generated in our model by varying structural changes in a sector. We have also found that differences between countries in industrial output over these long periods (shown in Figure 1) can also be generated on our macro model simply by varying the rate of structural change, after the same technical assumptions of new investment in industry. This defines how the market operates in the market place.

So, even if identical levels of investment of the same technical quality are going into industry each year, one can generate very different growth rates in the economy by varying the parameters that specify how the economy operates both in the market place and as affected by social policy.

What I want to emphasize is that technical change affects growth significantly in the very long term, but there are other factors on the social side that affect growth as much, and even more: how the economy is organized; the scope for incentive; how policies are operated by governments; if one ignores these factors one is disregarding a very large part of the growth process and of what should be meant by technical change.

Table 1 shows the results of a large questionnaire study in which we talked to a large number of businessmen and technical people in a large number of fields about labour productivity development in various production processes over a long period, and one can see the various rates of change that were estimated by these people. On the whole, we estimated that on average, labour productivity in the most efficient plants with new investment has been increasing only by some 2.5 per cent a year, over the twenty years between 1955 and 1975, even with the competition faced by Swedish industry. This should be compared with an aggregate rate of productivity change of about 6 to 7 per cent over the same period; a substantial difference that structural adjustment probably does much to explain.

Now let us return to the role of electronics in this process. It should be emphasized that to link microeconomics to macroeconomics one has to go by way of something that can be measured, and that it is possible to measure what is called 'technical change' at the company level.

In general, it seems from the case studies carried out both at my Institute and by the Computer and Electronics Committee that electronics is becoming very important in guiding the flow of production in a factory. We have found several cases where enormous productivity gains have been made simply by reorganizing production flow, without any new machinery or new gadget being installed. This shows that to obtain this sort of gain it is not necessarily the hardware that counts, but the organization of material flow round a plant. In several cases we have found electronics stores control systems keeping control of inventories so that goods can be found when needed, and unnecessary inventory kept to a minimum.

On the hardware side, the direct use of electronics in the production process in robots, automated production, and so on has been held back by a number of things. Mechanical technology is lagging behind sensor equipment, for example. But above all there is a knowledge of the various aspects of the production process which has for a long time been distributed around a plant or factory among

Table 1 Examples of labour productivity change in new plants
1955–1975

Industry	Productivity measure	Annual percentage change		
		1955–1965 (1)	1965–1975 (2)	1955–1975 (3)
Extractive industries				
Iron ore industry	Tons of rock/man hour	7.9	3.4	5.6
Forestry (logging)	m³/working day	7.2	11.6	9.4
Raw material processing				(5.9)
Pulp and paper industry	Tons/man hour	11.6	0–3.4	5.6–7.4
Ethylene production	Tons of ethylene /man hour	14.5	6.0	10.2
Intermediate goods				(3.0)
Commercial steel	Tons of crude steel/ man hour	6.0	4.8	5.4
Steel pipes	Tons/man hour	3.6	5.8	4.7
Steel forging	Tons/man hour	6.5	2.5	4.5
Investment goods				(2.6)
Heat exchangers	m² of heat absorbing surface/man hour	7.2	7.2	7.2
Hydro-power generators	MVA/man hour	1.0	3.6	2.2
Marine turbines	kW/man hour	7.2	−4.5	1.2
Shipbuilding	Tons of steel/man hour	7.2	1.0	4.1
Consumer goods				(0.4)
Pharmaceuticals	Tons/man hour	1.4	2.5	1.9
Food industry				
Canning and freezing	Tons of finished goods/man hour	13.1[a]	4.3	5.4
Sugar industry	Tons of beets/man hour	2.7[b]	4.1	3.4

[a] Refers to 1960–1965.
[b] Refers to 1960–1970.
Source: B. Carlsson and G. Olavi, 'Technical Change and Longevity of Capital in a Swedish Simulation Model', in G. Eliasson (ed.), *A Micro-to-Macro Model of the Swedish Economy*, IUI Conference Report 1978: 1, IUI, Stockholm 1978.

often highly skilled personnel, and it is very difficult to develop this and bring all the skills together so that a centralized computer can duplicate the process. This demonstrates that what is often called the software side, and what economists call 'human capital', often poses an important restriction on the application of electronics, reducing it to slower rates than one would expect on reading some of the publications on the subject.

As an analogy, Gutenberg invented the printing process several hundred years ago, and that was as revolutionary a technology as electronics is now. But printing was not generally applied and used on a large scale until enough people could read and write, and that took a long time. That is the 'human capital' aspect.

One thing we have learned is that the introduction of electronics techniques at factory or plant level is very piecemeal. One cannot, so to speak, automate the whole production chain immediately, one does it step by step. At each step of the automating process there may be a tremendous effect on the productivity of that production step, but at the overall factory level the effects of automation are only gradual, and not faster than productivity gains from earlier changes in technology. We have found a number of cases where larger effects on total factory productivity have been obtained by conventional means than have been gained from electronics.

Technical change, as measured by traditional macroeconomic methods, has resulted in the conclusion that it has been labour saving in character, rather than capital saving—at least in the post-war period until recently. But we have found that the introduction of electronics into Swedish industry has resulted in changes which are more capital saving than labour saving. Admittedly this is a conclusion that I have not entirely accepted as yet, because some of the measurement techniques are not exactly what one would like to see used, but we have seen it happen and people have pointed it out to us. The saving in capital is not usually in machinery but in better monitoring, keeping down inventories, outstanding debts, etc. These can mean sizeable improvements in profitability for companies if used intelligently.

One important question is whether this new technology will mean a general increase in the rate of technical change as compared to the past. We have found no evidence to suggest that this is necessarily the case. We may be wrong, but it is not obvious at all that it is true, which of course leads to the conclusion that we may be able to use the past to assess logically the future macro effects of the new technology.

One new aspect is the realization that electronics is a universal technology with many applications in all countries. We have found in our simulation experiments that if a country is lagging behind in technology, it is affected in terms of unemployment by the faster development of the same technology in other countries. The effects of the new technology in other countries are transmitted to the stragglers by international trade, price cuts, etc. And if the effects of new technology come to a country in that way, the effects on unemployment and growth are much harder than if the technology had been adopted by domestic industry. Thus if one is going to be concerned about the effects of these technologies on employment, one should worry about other countries taking the lead in introducing these economies, rather than one's own country.

We found in our simulation experiments that in the long run the main practical effects are more or less growth in income in the economy. In the short term one may find the expected effects on employment, namely that the acceleration of technical change through electronics produces more employment and not less, and vice versa. But the long term macroeconomic effects are very small and disappear quickly. On the other hand, the structure of employment is changing. People move between firms and change jobs within firms. Technological change tends to force this change in structure, as all other technological change has done, but that is nothing new: it has been happening all the time in Sweden for the last hundred years, and in most other countries.

8 Discussion

KEITH PAVITT
Senior Fellow, Science Policy Research Unit,
University of Sussex, UK

The electronics sector is the most fundamentally important industry of the seventies and eighties. That is obvious from several of the papers presented by people from the industry, both from Europe and Japan. It is the breathtaking pace of the changes in costs, reliability, and innovation which set microelectronics apart from other industries.

I must, in passing, disagree with Professor Reese, who argued that the pace of technical change is determined by the social relations of society, the 'power structure' as he would have it. I believe the pace of technological change in semiconductors and microelectronics is determined by what science and technology can offer. If the power structure could have determined the pace of technical change over the last decade, people would surely have ensured that we had an equivalent rate of change in energy. They would have ensured that we did not become so reliant on expensive Middle East oil and on OPEC as we have done.

The 'power structure', and that includes industry and government, is not yet able to stimulate such a rapid rate of technological change in the energy industry. This is because our understanding of the basic technology and the possibilities for change are different in the energy and electronics industries.

This having been said, I think the rapidly developing electronics industry clearly shows enormous possibilities for applications. We heard earlier about the two 'C's—computers and communications; in another context, we also heard about the three 'E's—electronics, exotic materials and energy. I am convinced that advances in the electronics sector could be harnessed to solve some of the wider economic and political issues and problems faced by Western societies. Many of these have been identified by the contributors— ways in which electronics could be applied to save energy; increasing the scope of and reducing the cost of communications; improving manufacturing processes. These would not necessarily destroy employment. On the contrary, they ought to create enormous investment and hence job opportunities.

My favourite anecdote for the future relates to the church clock being transformed into a wristwatch. Thus, what had been a public service, the church clock, has been taken over by and transferred to a private commodity—the wristwatch. One can see many possibilities in the future for various public services, particularly in information processing and education, being superseded by consumer durables through the convergence of telecommunications, the computer and television. This will happen both in the home and the office.

This pointer for the future leads me on to the second point I wish to make. But before doing so, I feel it needs to be stressed that we are still living in the dark. We are in the middle of a revolution, and at this stage it is extremely difficult to know exactly what is happening. The point I would make is that nobody—be they academics, industrialists, economists or technologists—can say at this stage with any degree of confidence just what the effect of this revolution will be on jobs, on the efficiency of manufacturing industry, or even on the size of industries.

I would remind you of two previous attempts at forecasting the possible implications of radical technical change. The first was during World War I with the introduction of radio. This was first of all seen not as a means of mass communication, but rather as a method of local communication, initially between ships, then between armies or groups within armies in the field, and eventually between private companies. It was only in the 1920s that the possibilities of radio as a means of mass communication were recognized. I think the pluralistic nature of the social system had a great deal to do with the spread of the use of radio; pluralism is even more important today.

The second example relates to the kind of predictions that were being bandied about in the early and mid-fifties about the development of markets for computers. Market forecasts for the uptake of computers looking just five years forward were wrong by a factor of ten. The predictions were ten times too low.

My proposition is that today we are equally in the dark when it comes to forecasting the effects of technical change. To put forward an intelligent policy for action, we must collect information on a much more systematic basis. We need better case studies from industry, from commerce, and better prepared macro-studies on what is actually happening, not on what is being predicted. Studies of the kind presented by Fujitsu, showing the rate of penetration of microelectronics in various products; studies of the sort being prepared in Sweden by Dr Eliasson's group. Only through such authoritative studies can we understand just what kind of revolution we are in, and in what direction it is heading.

The third point relates to my being somewhat confused about one of the recurring themes of the presentations; the relative strengths and weaknesses of Japanese technology. I have heard it said by both Europeans and Japanese that Japanese technology has not been particularly original. We know the story that in the 1950s and 1960s Japan was a very effective imitator of foreign technology. Japanese companies bought lots of licences for technologies already operating in other countries, and improved them. Some of the papers presented here, by both European and Japanese delegates, suggest that this is still the case—that the Japanese are still not strong in basic techno-logical research. Their *forté*, we are told, is still picking up innova-tions from other countries, improving them, developing them for their own purposes, scaling them up or down as required, and even completely re-engineering them to meet the needs of mass pro-duction. Sociologists suggest that the reason for this is that radical inventions require radical individuals, and the 'consensus decision-making process' prevalent in Japan means that the development of such radical individuals is not encouraged. If this 'weakness' in the Japanese system continues, innovation will never be a strong point in Japan.

At the same time, Europe wants, even needs, to learn things from Japan. What are these things? I would also like to enquire whether the Japanese are interested in allowing others to know in depth about their particular technological strengths? I am dubious about this apparent lack of innovative capacity in the Japanese system. It seems to me that many of the advances that one recognizes as important in the electronics industry are 'systems innovations'. Systems in products, systems in relating products to processes, electronic systems for improving the home, the office and, just as important, the factory. And it appears that the consensus approach is not so bad when it comes to developing systems. One only has to look at the string of successes from Japan to appreciate this. I would certainly like to clear up some of these apparent contra-dictions and ambiguities and hope that in the following pages we may glean exactly where Japanese technology may be heading in the future.

My fourth point relates to policy, and it will probably be con-sidered an outrageous argument coming from someone who used to work for the OECD, an organization dedicated to free trade. But

I feel that given the importance of electronics technology, it is completely unrealistic to expect that the economic laws of comparative advantage, as set out in textbooks and outlined in discourses at international conferences, are going to be allowed free play. They were allowed to work in the past in all the other major industries, such as steel, machine tools, and motor cars. One country normally had an advantage. But the point is that in the early stages of all these sectors there were clear leaders.

More recently we have seen, for example in computer technology, that other countries have not allowed the early and almost monopolistic lead held by the USA to continue. By various means—giving their companies subsidies or erecting protectionist barriers—other countries began to build up their own computer industry. The interesting pointer for the future in this context is just how Japan will react. Will it develop a more international stance as regards its computer sector?

In the past there is no doubt that Japan practised, extremely successfully, 'infant industry' policies. By that I mean it protected its own markets for new technology products while they were in their infancy and while they learned about the foreign competition and built up their own manufacturing and marketing strengths. Japan was a follower in most of the major waves of investment and innovations that I have mentioned earlier. The leaders tended to be in Europe and the USA. I wonder if this will be the case with electronics? Will the Japanese be followers or leaders in the development of this important new technology and investment opportunity? If they become leaders, I fear they might have a few painful lessons to learn. How will Japanese companies react to Americans or Europeans stealing or imitating their technologies or inventions? How will the others learn to imitate Japanese technology? Will they be successful? To what extent will they be able to absorb foreign technologies and possibly work practices?

Here are surely some interesting contradictions and challenging problems. The Europeans may also have to learn, and possibly copy, Japan's method of coordinating industrial policies. We hear a great deal about the Japanese support programme for very large scale integration (VLSI) technology. Should (or could) Europe follow a similar path? Would such a policy be appropriate for Europe?

These are just some topics to stimulate our discussion.

MICHIYUKI UENOHARA
Managing Director,
Nippon Electric Co. Ltd., Japan

In reply to Keith Pavitt's third point concerning the relative strengths and weaknesses of Japanese technology, let me reverse the question and relate how we in Japan perceive European attitudes and technologies.

We think Europeans are very strong in innovating 'seed' technologies, but somewhat weak in developing these for the benefit of mankind. Japan, on the other hand, is extremely adept at the practical exploitation of known and developed technologies, and even better at exploiting 'seed' technologies. We are aware of these differences, and consider on many occasions and in many committees and working groups how we can diversify and change these attitudes.

Many Japanese see the 'conservativeness' of the national character as a major cause of this lack of innovative ability. Others disagree with such a simplistic analysis. I feel that the environment in which we Japanese have lived in the past has had a big influence on our technological development. Overall, Japan has been a peaceful country, and environmental conditions are not harsh. We have at times been isolated from other continents and have had few wars with neighbouring countries. The relatively small population we had before the Meiji age ensured sufficient food for all the population. This fostered a conservative attitude in the people, and any changes have been evolutionary rather than revolutionary.

More recently, we realized that we needed more technology to change with the times. Naturally, we started looking to other countries, Western countries, for solutions. We adapted these in many instances, made them better and more suited to our needs and culture. We wanted to bring these changes about quickly, so we needed to learn as much as possible from others. In the process, Japanese society and the environment changed greatly. We have experienced a population explosion and now cannot support ourselves from our own resources. We have become very dependent on others for energy, be it coal, oil, or nuclear. In future, anything could happen: things are very unstable. We have many social problems and we have to tackle these in our own way. We cannot wait for others to solve the problem and show us how it has been done.

One aspect of this position is an urge to overcome these problems through the development of new technologies such as electronics, which could also help other nations. That is what we are talking about. We think we can and we certainly want to contribute in some way. We do not pretend to have all the answers. We know we have to rely on Europe and the USA to come up with new technologies that we can refine, adapt and improve. At the same time, we should be able to contribute our quota of technologies and techniques that could be adapted by other nations if they wished to do so.

The crux of my argument is that, because the Japanese social environment has changed so dramatically during recent years, I think we will in the future be challenging others in being first with new technological innovations.

GUNNAR ELIASSON
*President, Industrial Institute for Economic
and Social Research, Sweden*

I would like to challenge several aspects of Keith Pavitt's provocative propositions. One of his arguments states that electronics might in some way change the technological leadership patterns between Japan, Europe and the USA, and on a fairly large scale. He maintains that to some extent this has already happened. I feel, however, that the very nature of this new technology is, as we have all agreed, universal. It is very difficult to be a technological leader in every field. I have difficulties in accepting that one geographical area in the industrial world could become a leader across a whole sector like electronics. There has to be a changing distribution, and this is really very normal, and particularly so in a sector such as this where things move so fast and new applications crop up all the time.

The other argument is that being a technological leader is not necessarily the same as being a leader in international trade. Yet Japan is already being talked about as unassailable in electronics. The suggestion that Europe and the USA should accept this and seek leadership in other fields not related to electronics is one I cannot accept.

Returning to the use of the term 'revolution', I do not know what it means in this context. Just how long can it go on? One thinks of a revolution in terms of a sudden change that occurs over a certain time. The emergence of a new technology to maturity can last a very long time. Much patience is required before it starts to affect production and produce economic benefits leading to sustainable profits and changing trade patterns.

I feel that this 'electronics revolution' we keep talking about will go on for a long time. And when we look back on what has happened, even though it will be possible to pinpoint a number of instances which were revolutionary, the overall effect will not be seen to have been so great, compared to all the other things that happened during the same time, or even in the past. So I would like to ask whether this electronics revolution really is so unique? In economic terms, just what are its special features? Can we use the experiences of the past to assess the implications of the changes that are being forced on us? Finally, to echo Keith Pavitt—are we really so much in the dark about electronics?

DENZIL DUNNETT
London Representative,
Scottish Development Agency

I wish to make a few comments from perhaps an unusual stand-point, namely that of an agency wishing to attract electronics companies to a part of Britain.

In considering cooperation between the Japanese and European electronics industries, I think that here, as in other sectors, there is, and always will be, a certain amount of cooperation, and there is also bound to be continued competition. That is true for companies within the same country and between countries. An example of this was the description of Japanese research into very large scale integration (VSLI). At certain levels, the leading Japanese companies were able to pool resources and collaborate; at other levels, they maintained their competition.

One has to recognize that while one looks forward to collaborating with our Japanese colleagues, there is going to be some fierce competition between us. That is after all the life blood of international trade—the way we run our economic system.

Returning to Keith Pavitt's third point, he noted that there were certain weaknesses and strengths on both the Japanese and the European sides and raised the question: 'What do Europeans wish to get from Japan?' Here, I would like to offer some comments on the reasons why we in Scotland welcome more Japanese investment, particularly in electronics; and I would like to comment on what we might have to offer them. I think this will also be relevant to the point that Gunnar Eliasson raised, since some of the advantages that we hope to derive from having a greater Japanese presence in Scotland are of a general character while others are, I think, specific to electronics.

Scotland certainly looks forward to benefiting from being subjected to some of the Japanese companies' management techniques. We admire the way in which Japanese industry has managed to overcome some of the contradictions that have impeded the progress in productivity in our industries. That of course applies to all industries, not just electronics.

There is another point which also applies to many industries concerning the proportion of resources a firm commits to research and development. I think that in general, Japanese companies spend more on their R&D budgets than is the norm in Britain. One of the lessons that we in Britain are slowly learning is that we will have to increase the proportion of our resources devoted to research and development to a level much nearer that found in Japan. Again, this is a general point, but one which is particularly relevant in electronics, where obviously R&D is vital.

There is another reason why we are keen to develop the electronics sector in Scotland, and why we are actively seeking a greater Japanese presence, and that is the key position of electronics in the total industrial scene. Here, I must concur with Keith Pavitt. There really is something essentially unique about the role of electronics, in the way that it could transform and help all other industries. For example, traditional industries in Scotland, such as textiles, have suffered a major decline, but we now realize that the application of electronics to such an industry could offer it renewed vitality. This could be true for many other of our industries that are at present declining. Although as has been stated we have to be prepared to see our older industries simply vanish, while we adapt to more modern technologies, I feel electronics could play a key role in modernizing industry as a whole. That is one reason why we are developing and encouraging electronics firms to thrive in Scotland. We are, I emphasize, particularly glad to see Japanese companies opting to come there. We know that thanks to their commitment to R&D, and to their management skills, the Japanese have gone a long way towards the ideal way of manufacturing electronics products, and the goods they produce will enable other local industries to establish a lead in the future.

It is not, I think, for me to say here what we have to offer them in return. But we know one of the main reasons why Japanese companies are looking to Scotland is because they want to establish a foothold in Europe. There is no hiding the fact that they are taking the European market very seriously, and they see a manufacturing presence in Europe as essential for the increase of their market penetration. There are naturally other reasons why our Japanese colleagues are coming, but to my mind that is the fundamental one, and it seems to me to be a reasonable balance. We in Scotland are looking forward to getting from the Japanese rather different things to those they are seeking from us, but it seems to be a very reasonable exchange and a reasonable basis for increased cooperation.

CYRIL SILVER
Directorate-General for Research,
Science and Education, Commission
of the European Communities

I feel that this discussion, as with many other recent commentaries on the subject, places far too much emphasis on the revolutionary versus evolutionary aspects of what is happening in electronics. If I am correct, we are wrong, for many reasons, in picturing this as a revolution at all.

The first of these is that revolutions are feared and generally resisted, whereas evolutionary processes are much more readily accepted. But if you look at the time scale, although science and technology have been developing very rapidly during the last fifty years, the applications that we are now talking about in industry, in our homes and in our offices have really been very slow to arrive. As has already been pointed out, even though the market for computers might have been under-estimated when the first market predictions were made, computers are only now beginning to permeate our lives to the degree to which many prophesied they would in the 1950s.

Similarly, if one looks at the changes taking place in our offices today, it is certain that very few use word processors to the extent that they could. There is a reluctance to change. There are doubts on the part of management regarding the value of change until it is fully demonstrated. There are doubts about the wisdom of investing in costly new equipment when it is known that there is yet more modern equipment about to come on the market.

This lengthens the whole process and leads to two things. First, it provides the industry with the stimulus for even more and faster product development. But it also means a better opportunity and more time adjustment. That adjustment, I suspect, will be a continuing process over the next several decades, and perhaps indefinitely—who knows?

This raises a point which Keith Pavitt did not mention: the effects on society. I suspect that the effects on society are overestimated, here as in many other fields.

Our responsibility is to put all these issues in a reasonable perspective. We should stress at every opportunity the slow pace of the changes, and not talk so freely about revolution. We should be talking of the possibilities this technology offers for increased job opportunities over the long term. This is much better than talking of massive job losses occurring quite suddenly. Keith Pavitt did not suggest the latter, but I have heard it mentioned elsewhere. This now brings me to a rather different but related point.

At a meeting in Paris some years ago I had the temerity to suggest that certain advantages in the Japanese economy could stem from the fact that they employed substantially fewer social scientists than did many other countries. That remark created, I believe, the only laugh of the day on that occasion. But behind that comment lies my next question. We have heard that the educational system in Japan not only produces graduates in much higher numbers in relation to the population, than is the custom in Western countries, but that the number of engineers among these graduates is also proportionately much higher. However, the number of pure scientists, who would normally go into fundamental research is proportionately lower than is the case in the West.

When one seeks an explanation for the relative strengths and weaknesses of Japan in relation to the West, to ascertain why they are better at adapting other people's technologies than at innovating themselves, one should ask to what extent this difference in educational patterns plays a part? And is it true that in Japan a much higher proportion of the best brains go into engineering than is the case in the West? If it is true, why do these outstanding students prefer engineering and the pure sciences to the humanities?

This is linked to another point—the question of management. I have the impression that in Japan the engineer reigns supreme. We do not often find in Japan that managers have followed a route that is becoming so widely accepted in Europe, and has been largely imported from the USA. This consists of going to university to study almost anything, but preferably economics, and then proceeding to something called 'business studies' which they feel automatically makes them suitable for top management posts. I have a suspicion that in Japan this is a very unusual way to get to the top in industry. Instead, the way is to train in engineering and learn almost all the jobs in the factory before getting into the management stream. If that is the way, I would like to know what we in Europe could learn from such a route to the board room.

THE JAPANESE EDUCATIONAL SYSTEM AND THE ROLE
OF THE ENGINEER IN THE MANAGEMENT OF FIRMS

KEICHI OSHIMA
Department of Nuclear Engineering,
University of Tokyo, Japan

As an engineer, I am hesitant to accept all Mr. Silver's observations, for obvious reasons. But I believe he is essentially correct in relation to the teaching of social sciences in Japan. After World War II, apparently, almost all Japanese economists were Marxists, so the government did not rely on them, and instead used engineers to help in their economic planning. I must add, however, that I do not know whether this is an absolutely accurate picture. The point I would emphasize is that I believe nearly all Japanese companies oriented towards high technology products are now headed by people with an engineering background.

We can trace this back to the start of the modernization of Japanese industry, about a century ago. Technology and engineering were seen as a crucial part of this industrialization, modernization, Westernization—whatever you wish to call it. This was reflected in the education system, with both science and technology taught in the most practical way possible, with little emphasis placed on theory. In Europe during this period these subjects were still very much the domain of the academic world. Our Japanese system was, and still is, very much more oriented towards production, and using technology, rather than creating new sciences. Thus in the minds of most Japanese, engineering, management and even economics, are very closely related.

LOUIS DE GUIRINGAUD
Former Minister of Foreign Affairs,
France

There seems to be some contradictions concerning the Japanese methods of management. Some of the contributors have suggested that the Japanese system of management is better, while others of our European colleagues have indicated that they believe there is little difference.

The experiences of the few Japanese companies established in Europe have been mentioned, and it certainly seems that they get better results in quality and productivity than those obtained by similar neighbouring European owned companies. But I do not think that evidence is conclusive. There is not one Japanese company manufacturing here in Europe on a scale sufficient to allow us to compare management styles.

Managing a plant of, say, a hundred or so employees is not really management. All small and medium sized enterprises do this, some well, others less well. The Japanese are clearly better in managing large companies and plants employing several thousands of people. In these cases, I am afraid it is not possible to transpose Japanese management styles either to Europe or to the USA. The techniques can be used as a basis, but we cannot imitate them. They are a consequence of historical events, Japan having jumped without transition from a predominantly feudal system to an industrial society in a fairly short time and with the old concept of allegiance of the serf to the sovereign and the duties of the sovereign to his vassals remaining to a large extent. They have found that their companies work more efficiently if the managers are more concerned, have a greater sense of duty to the welfare of both employees in the factories and the executives, and when the workforce fully support the objectives of the company. This is an historical circumstance, and neither Europe or the USA could possibly set up such a condition now. In Europe, the struggle of the working classes against their employers has, in many cases, left too many divisions between the two sides. That kind of struggle did not exist in Japan, which is reflected in the differences between the two societies, and their attitudes to work.

Concerning the point about engineers, when I was ambassador to Japan, I carried out a similar investigation to the one described by Keichi Oshima. All the information I collected tended to show that Japan really does produce more trained engineers and technicians than we do in Europe.

There is a second fact which shows the difference between Japanese engineers and their European counterparts. Young Japanese engineers graduating from the best universities are immediately put to work when they join a company on projects in the factories. Whatever degrees they might possess, whatever schooling they have had, they start to learn practical jobs right away. If they are in the steel industry, they will spend two years working in a blast furnace or rolling mill. They are then in direct contact with the supervisory staff and the workers, and during this period their wages are not much different from those earned by the lower supervisory staff.

In France, and I suspect the same is true for Germany and Britain, students with degrees from universities, polytechnics, or higher engineering schools just do not go to work in a rolling mill or start operating a blast furnace. They go straight up to the executive offices to work on administration, planning, or 'management sciences'. This is the difference and one has to understand it to explain why the Japanese management system apparently gets so much more from their workforce. The point is that when these young engineering graduates start rising in the hierarchy, they can still be in touch with the workforce and the supervisory staff. They have a much better appreciation of what the workers' problems are, they find it easier to talk to them and to enlist their cooperation with unaccustomed procedures or changes when these appear necessary.

Another aspect concerns retraining facilities. These engineers play a key role in the constant modernization process to boost productivity and efficiency. There is a constant exchange of views between the workers, managers and supervisory staff. This makes the engineer even more useful to the company. This is how Japanese engineers and managers are trained, and we in Europe have to admire it. This is why they are so good at improving on the patents they acquire, why they seem to be able to improve productivity and quality almost continuously.

At a somewhat lower level than that of the engineer, there is another very important difference between Japanese and French attitudes. This is the wide gap that exists between supervisory staff and workers. I suspect it is even deeper in other European countries, notably Britain, but it does not exist in Japan. The working team there is very much more cohesive, and this is a reflection of the importance of the supervisory staff—the foremen— in Japanese factories. It is very important to ensure this dialogue between workers and the company, and this consensus that we all admire in Japan but lack in Europe is a prerequisite, and one of the major factors, in the industrial success of Japan.

Of course this 'consensus' approach cannot be transferred as such, but we in Europe can draw lessons from it. First and foremost, it is clear that the training of engineers and the number of scientific and engineering graduates must be increased. We have made progress towards this in France over the last few years, but certainly not enough. There has been, and still is, a tradition of literary, legal and what I would call 'human' studies in Europe, which has led to erudite 'honest gentlemen'. It is those with this kind of education who gain access to power. This attitude is still being perpetuated. For example, in France, the National School of Administration is a 'nursery' of leaders of industry and government, and its curriculum is still broadly inspired by classical studies—humanities, law and economics. We have to accept this tradition, while pointing to it as an explanation for one of the fundamental differences between the Japanese and French systems.

There are other things we can learn from the Japanese about the training of engineers. We must ensure that our young engineering graduates get more practical experience early on in their careers, and make it easier for them to mix with workers and supervisors. Another lesson to be learnt is the importance of the cooperation and participation of shopfloor workers in decision making. Some tentative efforts have been made in this direction, perhaps more in Germany than in France or Britain.

There is another important factor that can explain the extra productivity achieved by Japanese companies, and I would call this the 'information factor'. As soon as something has been discovered or produced in Japan, it is published and disseminated. It would be interesting to know just why this is so. There is tradition, of course, but I would say that the attitude of the major industrial groups and huge trading companies plays an important part in this. They feel it is in their own interests to publicize, both internally and throughout the world, knowledge that they have discovered. They also feel it is in the interests of their customers.

Yet another dimension is the role of the government, through the auspices of the Ministry of International Trade and Industry (MITI). This has no equivalent in the world and its very name explains its objectives: industry must serve foreign trade. MITI itself encourages the dissemination of information on new discoveries in Japanese companies and government-funded research establishments. I am not sure this is the same for other administrations. Certainly it is not the case in France. Here, we have traditions that are exactly the opposite to this. The administration guards and retains information as a matter of course, and it is very difficult to break down such traditions. These then are the kind of lessons that we, the French, can learn from Japan.

MARC DUPUIS
The University of Paris,
France

My first observation concerns the number of engineers in Japan. If you add up the number of students registered in engineering faculties, economics faculties or studying business administration, it comes to about 60 per cent. I do not have the exact figures, but I would say the distribution is 25 per cent in engineering, and the balance split about equally between the other two disciplines. The number of students studying pure sciences, on the other hand, is very low, about 5 per cent. The remainder study medicine, literature and pharmacy.

If we look at France, we find the position quite the reverse. Universities mainly produce scientists trained for pure research. Since 1958 they have started to train engineers, but the major responsibility for the training of our engineers rests with the Higher Engineering Schools, and the places available at these is still low. The system is geared to train an élite, and not to train large numbers of engineers for production management.

In the élitist centres of knowledge in Japan, such as the former Imperial University or the private universities, the number of students in the faculty of technology is much higher than the number of students studying sciences. This is due to the general attitude that for a young Japanese student, it is considered quite as brilliant and glorious to be a technologist as to be a scientist. This is not the attitude in France, which is that intellectually, pure knowledge will always prevail over good technology.

Now I wish to make an observation about the debate concerning the evolutionary or revolutionary nature of electronics. In France, we are getting quite used to reading in newspapers and the technical press reports of what is happening in Japan. They invariably give the impression that a revolution has in fact occurred there and that the Japanese are far ahead of Europe in technology. I have lived a great deal of my life in Japan, and I was always struck with the fact that the introduction of electronics in Japan has been a rather subtle process. In Europe during the 1970s, the first impact of electronics was its use in data processing. Thus, the French were trying to find high-powered tools for scientific calculations and to use computers to solve elaborate management problems. Conversely, in Japan the first application of computers and data processing was for process control; for improving the efficiency of chemical and manufacturing plants and for data transmission. Data transmission was taken up enthusiastically by many Japanese companies. One of the first major applications for the man in the street was for booking airline or theatre tickets and for banking. It then spread further and further.

The point I wish to make is that electronics was developed in Japan with a social purpose in mind. In Europe, I am afraid, as with education, we approached the whole business with an aristocratic, intellectual, somewhat highbrow outlook. The application of technology has always been much more pragramatic in Japan, and oriented towards applications with a strong social purpose. Of course,

Europeans and American companies often say the same: that the products they have developed are primarily for the good of society —but I wonder whether this is not just an advertising gimmick.

ALEXANDER KING
Chairman, The International Federation
of Institutes for Advanced Study

The question of 'strength' and 'weakness' is an extremely important topic to consider from the point of view of both sides, if we really are talking about two sides. The OECD countries have very many examples of these differences and there are many important cultural differences between the countries of the OECD. The point made earlier, that the Europeans were good at innovating and the Japanese better at applications, has of course been related to the European and American situations, right from the time of the World War II. I remember very well making similar comparisons at that time between the UK and the USA, showing that for every basic research worker in the USA, there were 2.5 people involved in applied research and development. The figures quoted for the UK were an unfavourable ratio of 1.1 engineer or applied scientist for every scientist doing basic research.

This meant that during the war, we in the UK had all kinds of bright ideas, most of which, even the military ones, were only exploited in the USA. Since then, this pattern has been inherited by Europe as a whole, and the American virtues and advantages seem to have passed to the Japanese.

It seems obvious to me that cultural factors in technological developments and innovations are extremely important, and we have not given nearly enough attention to them. I am sure that the Japanese, with their lack of interest in sociology, have not done so well in that field. However, I should add that the social science scene in Japan is of great interest to me. A few years ago, I was a member of a small delegation from the OECD which spent a short time in Japan studying that country's policy towards the social sciences. We were astonished to find that although the number of post-graduate degrees in subjects like sociology, anthropology, political sciences and economics was fairly high, it was completely overshadowed by the number of post-graduate students studying the sciences and engineering. This is obviously reflected in the realities of economic life.

One must also remember that in Japan there is a tremendous respect for the generalist, in government service, in industry and in all subjects, be they arts or sciences. A very important aspect of life there is the way young graduates enter industry and proceed by promotion and many internal movements up the managerial ladder. This is considerably supported by very good in-house training. We in Europe tend to put very much less emphasis on in-house training schemes.

To return to the role of engineers, another important difference concerns the 'status' factor. In Japan, and to some extent in Germany, the status of engineers in society is very high, and has been for a long time. The situation is quite the reverse in Britain where, partly for historical reasons, we use the word 'engineer' for anyone from a technician or plumber to a highly qualified, top level applied physicist. This has meant that engineers in Britain are at a disadvantage compared with accountants, lawyers and other professionals in the competition for top jobs in even the largest industrial concerns. These cultural aspects are, I believe, very important when we compare the industrial positions of Japan and Europe.

During the so-called 'industrial revolution' in Britain, the engineer had a very high status and was regarded as a leader in society, especially in Scotland, where much of the early industrialization took place. As scientists like Maxwell came along with important new discoveries, this attitude slowly dissipated and a certain academic élitism in favour of scientists at the expense of engineers crept into the system. This had a very detrimental effect on industrial development.

But what has this to do with the microelectronics revolution? I will explain, but first I cannot resist adding my own views on this debating point of 'revolution' versus 'evolution'. I think much of our difficulty here is one of semantics. The first industrial revolution was in fact also an evolution. It took decades to flower and the present development of microelectronics is just the same. What we see in industrial and social development, or evolution, is several discontinuities occurring from time to time. The invention of the steam engine was one such discontinuity. It led to a tremendous number of new activities and applications. In the textile industry, it started a whole new wave of mechanization; in mining, it made possible the draining of water from coal seams, leading to dramatic improvements in safety and productivity, and led to a host of new industries. Similarly, microelectronics is another discontinuity, with its universality and wide range of applications. I believe it is 'revolutionary' to the same extent as the invention and harnessing of the steam engine.

This first industrial revolution did not create social changes overnight. There were many difficulties, for example those created by the Luddites, who feared change and thus destroyed new machinery as it was being introduced. Social changes took many decades to work through, and I think the same is happening now. There will clearly be extremely profound social changes as a consequence of the microelectronics revolution, but we will not see them occur tomorrow.

My plea is that we should try and identify the possible social, economic and environmental changes, and prepare for them in advance, if that is possible. The first industrial revolution was horribly mismanaged and led to tremendous suffering, much of which was completely unnecessary. To take a very simple example: London was growing very rapidly as a consequence of people moving in from the country looking for work, and this led to very poor living conditions. The death rate rose tremendously during the first decade of the last century. The situation was even worse in some other early industrial cities like Glasgow and Manchester.

The situation could and should be very different today. If one considers cities that are expanding very rapidly today, such as Mexico City, one will see that much of the increase is coming from within the city itself. We have better conditions today, and more knowledge. We ought to be able to avoid many of the difficulties that occurred during that previous revolution, including the temporary problem of lack of employment. In Europe, too, there are bound to be many conflicts between the need for improving productivity and the possible effect of this on employment. But we should anticipate these problems now, and to a large extent alleviate them, by providing better social benefits and bringing about changes in the nature of society, which ought to take place in any case.

As regards the next stage in microelectronics, I feel it should concentrate much more on new applications and modifications to existing industry, rather than on a host of new innovations for the consumer. The new technical advances should aim to make industry more automated, manufacturing equipment 'intelligent' and devise new forms of transportation. This is bound to create social unrest, and I think Japan will be able to make the transition to this much more automated industrial society far better than the USA or Europe. The consensus approach that has been mentioned so often ought to help it overcome the inevitable social difficulties created, for it has conditioned the Japanese to accept changes smoothly and without undue social unrest. The Japanese are disciplined and hard working, they are marvellous at imitating and improving on the discoveries of others, and they have a paternalistic approach which allows society to absorb structural unemployment in a variety of ways. Japanese companies will, I am sure, lead the way in developing other electronic innovations, which will help them overcome any unemployment problems in the future. In Japan, it will be the companies, large and small, that will tackle the problem of jobs, while in Europe that will be left to governments to solve. The country's extremely harmonious industrial relations, and the good contacts and understanding between government and industry, also favour Japan.

In summary, I think Japan can look forward to a very prosperous future. We in Europe will have much to learn from Japan, but I fear we will be bogged down with too much internal dissension and discussion to solve the problems. I think that because of our historical traditions our cultural development will lead us in different directions from those taking place in Japan.

PART II: MICROELECTRONICS IN EVERYDAY LIFE

Introduction

LOUIS DE GUIRINGAUD
Former Minister of Foreign Affairs,
France

Day after day we see more clearly that the technologies involved in this new branch of industry will have a revolutionary impact on the world in which we live. Indeed, the revolution brought about by the miniaturization of equipment, the standardization of electronic components and the continued reduction in prices will make it possible to integrate more and more intelligence into the equipment found in homes, offices and factories. Many industrial products will be entirely changed; the design and entire concept of certain products will be totally overhauled and hence daily life, and in particular working conditions, will be transformed. These changes in our daily life, brought about by microelectronics, pose many cultural, industrial, economic and social problems.

How can we re-utilize manpower which the automation of productive means will make superfluous in manufacturing? How can we increase the production of software? How can we adapt education provided in primary and secondary schools and universities? What will be the impact of these new technologies on the centralization or decentralization of our societies? Will the new technology engender social upheaval? These are all challenging questions. It has been suggested that the appearance of electronics will bring about a change in the evolution of history comparable to the changes brought about by the steam engine, electricity and the combustion engine. Some people even think that these changes will be even greater than those experienced during the Industrial Revolution and that microelectronics, in particular, will provide a new dimension to our civilization.

We could, in fact, compare this change to the transformation of our old rural societies which follow the appearance of machinery and fertilizers in agriculture and which brought about a tremendous increase in crop yields—at the same time, emptying our countryside and initiating the flight to the cities. Microelectronics may bring about a shift of labour which is now working in our factories to the service sector of the economy. Will it bring about the creation of as many jobs as it eliminates? Will it be possible to re-educate a large enough proportion of this labour force which is thereby freed, or should we accept the fact that a sudden and dramatic change will be one of the essential components in the creation of unemployment in industrial countries?

I cannot claim to be able to answer these questions personally. I merely wish to raise them in the context of the following papers, which will, I hope, cast new light on some of the principal issues. Clearly the possible changes may prove beneficial as well as harmful and so we concentrate first on a precise definition of the problems. Secondly, we attempt to bring to the fore factors which will ensure that these inevitable changes will prove beneficial to the world in which we are going to live in the coming years.

SABURO OKITA
Former Minister of Foreign Affairs,
Japan and Advisor to the Japan
Economic Research Centre

One of the major questions is whether the use of microelectronics will increase unemployment. Some time ago I had occasion to talk with a European friend who said that while microelectronics may create employment in Japan it may create unemployment in Europe. I hope this will not be the case. Eventually we should be creating employment in both areas.

Somewhat related to this is the question of the impact of microelectronics on international trade. We have already seen the so-called trade friction between Japan and Europe, and between Japan and the USA. Some of this friction has been generated in the area of electronics. We have to find a solution to these problems because Japan has to exist harmoniously with other countries, otherwise she will have very serious problems.

There is also the question of the impact of microelectronics on the future of developing countries. The future of the Third World is a major concern. Broadly speaking, there are two types of impact that this new technology might have on the future of the Third World. One is that microelectronics may replace human labour with electronic machinery. In the past the economists have argued that when the rich industrial countries increase wages, the poorer low income countries with an abundant labour force and relatively low wages will take over the labour intensive industries and this will create a new international division of labour. Now, with the emergence of electronics we see that sometimes robots and electronic automation can provide cheaper and more accurate high quality labour than the labour in poorer countries. This may have serious implications for the future of the economies of developing countries.

Another possibility is that the use of microelectronics may bring about more efficient means of educating people in developing countries, which will improve the quality of labour in those countries and create the possibility of introducing audio-visual educational systems even in very remote areas. This may enhance the potential of many people in such countries and may improve their position.

We do not know which factor will be more dominant in the future in the context of the influence microelectronics will have on the people of the Third World, but we should try to bring about a positive, beneficial effect rather than a negative one.

As I mentioned earlier, if electronics is to produce employment in Japan alone while creating unemployment in other parts of the world, then Japan herself cannot survive economically and politically. We should make a joint effort to bring about a positive benefit from microelectronics all over the world, both in industrialized countries and the Third World.

9 Perspectives on the microelectronics industry and technology in Japan

Takemochi Ishii, Faculty of Engineering,
University of Tokyo, Japan

In looking at the development of technology from a macroscopic, historical point of view, we see that in the 1920s and 1930s technological revolutions occurred in the electricity, automobile, chemical and aircraft industries. From the 1940s to the 1960s the areas of change were in transistors, computers, television, nylon, jet engines, rockets and penicillin.

Blocks of innovation occurred at roughly fifty to sixty year cycles, leading to accompanying economic cycles with a similar period. The existence of such cycles was discovered by Kondratiev, and the Austrian economist Schumpeter named the phenomenon the 'Kondratiev wave'. According to this theory, technological innovation would lose momentum from the middle of the 1970s and would not start up again until the twenty-first century. This was the accepted view in Japan until a few years ago, but has recently changed.

The future of industry based on the Kondratiev model looked gloomy, because it was seen to be entering a trough as far as technological innovation was concerned. Moreover, Japan is said to lack creativity in the area of technological innovation and this led to pessimism. On top of this the oil crisis of 1973 hit Japan, which lacks natural resources, very hard. Towards the end of the 1960s the pollution problem became serious, triggering public criticism of industry and technology, and the high economic growth rate of 10 per cent suddenly declined. As a result Japanese industry faced a crisis.

Recognizing the changes in economic circumstances, industry tried to cope with these changes with several measures that were put decisively into action. Companies moved into pollution prevention technology and energy saving technology at world levels. Fortunately the high growth necessary to establish the basic technological industries (electric utilities, iron and steel, petrochemicals, automobiles, home appliances, etc.) after the war had already been achieved, and Japan had a foundation on a par with other advanced countries. New production facilities had been established and we had a young and flexible workforce.

From 1975 the Japanese economy recovered from its dangerous stall and moved into an orbit of steady growth. During this period, however, there were decisive changes in the structure of industry, and also a qualitative change. The industrial structure changed from a quantity-oriented material industry, because of market saturation, to a quality-oriented process industry. The innovation in production systems in the material industry has, of course, also occurred with a view to changing from quantity to quality. These changes can, in short, be expressed by saying that Japan no longer adhered to the notion that large is beautiful.

What then represents this newly emerging era? The symbol of the new age is large scale integration—LSI. In the late 1960s integrated circuits were beginning to be used in computers and electronic appliances. But the impact of LSI after 1976 is truly striking. As you know, LSI is a tiny chip, 5 mm square and symbolized the 'small is beautiful' concept. The number of functions that could be put on one chip at the beginning of the 1960s was two transistors, six resistors and two capacitors. By the 1970s the level of integration had gone up so much that from 7000 to 10000 devices could be fitted on to one chip. The 100000 device chip has now arrived, and the trend is still continuing: the age of very, very large scale integration can be expected.

This improvement in integration in semiconductor chips has produced a change in quality rather than quantity, and this has had a profound effect on industry as a whole. As a result of integration the reliability of electronic circuits has improved exponentially. High performance is available even under severe conditions, such as in vehicles or in machine tools. In addition, the small size, light weight, and low power consumption make it easier to incorporate electronics in various machines, including portable, battery driven devices. Because integrated circuits can be mass produced, incredible cost savings have been achieved. For example, the cost of the 65k bit dynamic RAM, a first generation of LSI circuit, has dropped by a factor of ten over the year 1981.

I have been looking at microelectronics, but I now want to take a broader look at Japanese industry from the technological point of view.

According to the OECD survey of 1977, the value added in money terms in the mechanical engineering sectors of various countries was as follows: USA, 35.8 per cent; Japan, 19.5 per cent; West Germany, 13.7 per cent; France, 7.7 per cent; Great Britain, 5.0 per cent;

Italy, 3.8 per cent. For the same countries, the proportion exported was: West Germany, 20.5 per cent; USA, 18.5 per cent; Japan, 17.2 per cent; France, 8.5 per cent; Great Britain, 7.9 per cent. As indicated by these figures, Japan is among the 'big three' in mechanical engineering. In 1979, 20.3 per cent of machinery was exported and 3.7 per cent imported. Mechanical engineering represented 10 per cent of Japan's GDP.

The figures emphasize the point that Japan is short of natural resources and must import food, raw materials, crude oil etc., and as a result must export finished products to balance exports and imports. The majority (about 60 per cent) of these exports come from the mechanical sector.

Let us now look at the effect of LSI on the mechanical sector. Today structural change in the industry has started. This must mean that the Kondratiev cycle no longer applies. There are indications that a new wave of different types of innovation is starting, not necessarily as predicted by Kondratiev. The Kondratiev cycle was arrived at inductively on the basis of the historical past, when technological change was based on available materials and power sources. The new media for distributing information were not taken into account. The reason is obvious: the electronic computers available from the 1940s to the 1960s were very primitive compared to present machines. They were more like prototypes or trial products compared to the computers backed up by today's software. In other words, the real development of software and information technology is only just beginning, and development up to now may be considered as almost preparatory.

Apart from VLSI, the outstanding innovations in information technology to be expected will be the Josephson junction, optical fibres, lasers, fine ceramics, amorphous solar cells, pattern recognition, digital image processing and a Japanese character (Kanji) word processor. Provided that these promising developments relating to information technology can be effectively applied to enhancing Japan's mechanical engineering products, the future looks bright. The word 'mechatronics' has been coined in Japan to describe this process.

From the standpoint of performance and costs, the conditions for the practical use of LSI on a large scale now exist in Japan. In fact there have been some remarkable developments in the field of 'mechatronics' as a result of active use of LSI. For example, in machine tools there is the numerically controlled (NC) machine tool, the machining centre, the flexible manufacturing system (FMS) and industrial robots that are in extensive use. Computer aided design (CAD) is put into practice in various plants, and computer aided manufacturing is also becoming a reality.

Some people have voiced the criticism that the new word 'mechatronics' is not necessary, and that there was another word, 'electromechanics' already in existence. But that would be to fail to give the impact of LSI on mechanical engineering its true significance, which is revolutionary. The use of a flexible manufacturing system may bring savings in manpower of a factor of 100. Quality will be higher, and quoted delivery times shorter and more credible, thus leading to reduced costs and lower break-even points.

Large scale integration has led to increases in performance of NC tools at decreasing prices with the result that NC tools are being used by small and medium-sized companies, and in consequence production is being spread among a greater number of firms. In a country where sub-contracting rates are high, this trend is expected to continue.

Let us now turn to the impact of mechatronics on industrial society.

The cost of energy as a proportion of production costs, as given in the economic White Paper of 1981, was over 3 per cent on average, but in the mechanical sector it was about 1 per cent. In the iron and steel industry the figure was 9 per cent; in paper and pulp 8 per cent; and in the chemical industry 6 per cent. Thus in comparative terms the mechanical sector has low energy costs.

Taking the growth in the mining and manufacturing industry as a base, the products that significantly exceeded the growth rate were video tape recorders (ten times); NC machine tools (less than ten times); industrial robots (seven times); integrated circuits (less than six times); facsimile machines (five times); and electronic calculators (five times). These figures suggest that mechatronics goods are beginning to show pre-eminent growth potential and at the same time, that these goods are comparatively cost-competitive against increases in raw materials or energy costs (especially crude oil).

Mechatronics is a fabrication industry, and consequently has high labour costs. As a result, the impact of the industrial robot and the NC tool will be felt on a large scale. Automation and labour saving will reduce the need for workers, but those that remain must be of the highest quality. It will be important for workers to have a knowledge of software; in other words, shopfloor work is now intellectual work. Fortunately, for Japan practically all her young people are high school graduates and 40 per cent of all Japanese are university graduates. As the educational level in Japan is so high,

I think we will be able to supply the personnel needed for the mechatronics industry of the future.

Of course, labour saving machinery may produce unemployment, but in Japan, at least, this has not happened. Most people think that this is no problem in the medium term, but it may be a problem in the long term. The Ministry of Labour and the Ministry of Industry and Trade have started a study, and the industry and trade unions have also started to show an interest. So far we have conditions in which we are able to accommodate this kind of change, and this is an advantage—due in the main to the nature of Japanese trade unions, which are formed in each company, and also because of the system of consultation before the introduction of new machinery.

It has also been possible to transfer people within a company to other posts. For example, people have been transferred to monitoring, surveillance or maintenance types of work, or to sales and service within the company. But some people fear that this ability to absorb redundant jobs may be lost in the long term.

Of course, mechatronics is a growth industry and so it can produce new jobs, which some say will counterbalance the jobs lost through labour saving. Overall this may be true, but there are people who will inevitably lose their jobs because of some labour saving and this could be a source of friction. There is also the question of women workers. As electronics production will be mainly brainwork, both men and women are equally suitable. This effectively doubles the available workforce.

So, in conclusion, what of the future? We need to develop our own technology and we need to produce new and innovative technologies. The government is starting to assist in this.

When we look to the future of industry and technology, what are the needs with the longest lead times? Personnel training is one, locations for factories is another. In Japan this is very important as suitable available land is very scarce in proportion to the size of the population. The Minister of Industry and International Trade is saying that Japan is a country that must base itself on technology. How does that affect strategy? Products must be of high added value and small LSI is a prime example—the price per ton is about $¥200 \times 10^9$, about the same as silver. It is suitable for transport by air, thus the factory must be near an airport. Production needs a very clean environment with lots of pure, clean water. At a time of rapid growth, the heavy chemical factories were built near the sea. Today the trend will be to build factories around airports. This also may lead to a U-turn in the movement of the population, away from the

cities and into the country, or to the provinces. Technology will be
will be distributed with the population, with provincial universities
taking a more prominent role.

10 The influence of microelectronics on the conception of products

Pierre Aigrain, Former French Secretary
of State for Research and Corporate
Managing Director of Thomson CSF, France

Microelectronics has begun to have a profound influence on industries other than those from which it originally stemmed, namely the electronics and telecommunications industries. It has achieved this by virtue of an improvement, or even a revolution, in the methods of manufacturing in, for instance, the mechanical industries.

Japan has a comfortable lead for which we should congratulate her, while regretting that Europe has not been able to keep up. Europe must catch up, but is now, as it were, running in pursuit of an already moving train. The revolution in microelectronics has yet further to go. It is not only fabrication methods which are going to be radically changed, but also their very design. In the coming years, machinery will change by a continuous process in the direction of more efficient manufacture and higher quality. The virtue of applying new manufacturing technologies and using computer aided design is the key concept. The very design of such products will be revolutionized.

Let me give you a few examples. The revolution has already begun to a certain extent, though for the time being it involves only particular products or sub-units which consumers do not always recognize as innovative. In the design of mechanical products, the engineers and companies involved were at every point in time under certain constraints. These constraints involved the materials used and the nature of the devices used to drive their equipment. Over the last hundred years there existed a whole body of doctrine, a teaching approach, methods which made it possible to select the best products with respect to these limitations. What is now beginning to happen with the introduction of microelectronics is a remarkable capacity for information processing at negligible cost. Incidentally, manufacturers complain about this because they find these products are not very expensive and it is not easy to make money with such products these days. The competition is such that manufacturers must adjust to this situation. Nevertheless, the possibilities provided by microelectronics have the indirect and not always noticeable effect of removing some of these limitations. Consequently, it becomes feasible to design products which would not have been possible before. It is not only a matter of improving products. In terms of their specifications, some new products would have been previously inconceivable.

The initial examples, as is often the case, are highly sophisticated products, in for instance the military field. Let me give you an example. Everyone has heard of the concept of centralized flight control, the so-called 'fly by wire technique'. This is basically very simple, involving the use of electronic devices for the aircraft control surfaces—for the rudder, elevators, wing flaps etc. They do not act directly, but receive indications of what the pilot wants to do and then they in turn alter the appropriate mechanical controls. This may not seem a very great innovation, but let me remind you that the first demonstration of an aircraft autopilot was in 1914 at an airshow in Le Bourget. The Sperry brothers demonstrated an aeroplane which flew automatically. The pilot, one of the Sperry brothers, walked out on the wing and the airplane kept on flying.

This is, therefore, not a new idea. But all automatic pilot systems and all control servo mechanisms for aircraft, until the last decade, involved electromechanical or hydromechanical devices. This meant they function rather slowly. They were of course faster than the pilot alone, but nevertheless not very swift compared to certain parameters characteristic of the aircraft's behaviour or response time. A consequence of this was that airframe manufacturers had to ensure that the aerodynamic behaviour of the plane would be suitable for all possible flight configurations, in particular for the critical landing phase. This meant rules, such as the centre of gravity being at a particular location: were this not the case, the aircraft might fly but prove unstable. Neither the servo mechanism nor the pilot could respond swiftly enough to deal with this instability. The introduction of microelectronics in aircraft made it possible for controllers to respond swiftly enough and to take into account every parameter which could have an influence on the aircraft's flight, including those observable from the pilot's seat and those measured with sensors. Using these sensors, and various calculations which are not very difficult with microelectronics, it became possible to eliminate constraints on the aircraft's operation.

It is not always clear whether removing such limitations have significant consequences for performance, as when one eliminates a particular constraint in a device, one can always find a new optimum operating condition. The new optimum is nearly always better than that previously achieved. In some cases, while retaining an equal performance level for the user, an aircraft can be reduced in weight by 30 per cent, using the fly by wire technique. (Of course, you can keep the same weight and improve performance levels.) These techniques are being used in modern military aircraft. They are used less in civil aviation because the security of civil aircraft should be higher than that of military craft. In war, the real danger is not of accidents, but of being shot down. Thus it is necessary to have a higher safety margin for civil aircraft resulting in the slower, more cautious introduction of such equipment.

These changes do not have a direct impact on the widespread consumer use of this equipment, although improvements in the performance of civil aircraft will have an impact for each of us since they reduce fuel consumption and costs. Nevertheless, the same kind of problem can be found in many different fields. Automobile engines for example derive more or less directly from the invention more than a century ago of the four-stroke engine (in 1878) and has, thanks to the efforts of generations of engine builders, reached a stage which we can deem to be a matter of technical perfection within the existing constraints. For some time we have known that it would be useful, in terms of performance levels, to increase compression and to reduce the running speed. Why then has this not been done? Basically the reason is that it would require a whole series of control devices to monitor the ignition as well as controlling the mixture of air and gas to be burnt. This could not be done using mechanical procedures within an accuracy range or a time constant range great enough to respond to the limitations of the system.

There are always limits related to the physical and chemical properties of the fuel mixture or the characteristics of the materials used. For instance, increasing compression encounters a limit—the high speed rattling of a motor. Knock in a motor is not very important when there is a low rotation speed; it is unpleasant, but not serious. When there is high speed knocking, it can destroy the engine within a few seconds. The introduction of electronic ignition and electronic control of the fuel/air mixture injected has made it possible to get within the knock limits without actually reaching them, because the ignition rate can be controlled with a wider range of parameters, taking into account all factors influencing this phenomenon. However, the engine responding to these new possibilities would no longer be the conventional engine. It is not only a matter of adapting by adding electronic ignition to a conventional automobile to get the greatest advantage from microelectronics; it would also prove advantageous in terms of reliability. The first car to be mass produced using this idea was the Citroen Visa, a cheap popular car. Here is a new technology which can be introduced into very simple products as opposed to complex items such as military aircraft. In this particular case I have been told that redesigning the engine using microelectronics made it possible to reduce fuel consumption by 15 per cent yet retiming the same performance.

These two examples now belong to the past—the recent past, but still the past. What I would like to emphasize is that we are now going to see many other examples: almost every product in the mechanical industries sector should be redesigned and rethought. This change will imply a completely different architecture for these products. In this respect we are starting to see examples in limited numbers. This is not really surprising as they involve mechanical products which have been traditionally manufactured by the electronics industry. Within the same companies one could find people working on mechanical products and electronic products. Let us take as an example a very simple product—the phonograph. This has an electric motor. Fifty years ago it used a clockwork mechanism. Later, they all had electric motors. Then there were automatic record-changing devices. All these functions used one and occasionally two electric motors which revolved regularly and carried out a series of complex functions. One involved the part which carried the record and the part which raised the arm, another was to shut down the motor when the record finished, while yet another was to trigger the device which let the next record down on the turntable, and so forth. All this was achieved by a complex, costly, sometimes unreliable series of cables, wires and gears.

The introduction of microelectronics in modern phonographs has led to a completely different design. There is still a motor, but perhaps the term 'motor' is no longer appropriate as it implies something which revolves. Some of these devices do not rotate, they are linear. Let us call them 'actuators' to use more up-to-date terminology. These actuators are quite different, depending on the motion to be achieved. There is, of course, a turntable motor, there is something to trigger the placing of the next record, and there is another control to lift or lower the arm. One solution involves a slow progressive movement which should be done without jerks. A special actuator is needed, involving a resistance wire. This heats up when a current passes through it and dilates. This, in turn, lowers the arm on the record. This design turns out to be not only less expensive and more effective, but also more flexible in use. It makes it possible to achieve things which were previously very difficult to carry out.

You can see what the implication of this example is. The developments in the design of phonographs were carried out by people who were accustomed to using microelectronics for other parts of a hi-fi system. This could and should be done for every product. I think there will be further development of every mechanical product. The advantages of this development are obvious, but we should not underestimate the problems involved.

Let us examine some of these problems, because they are much more numerous and complex than generally believed. The most difficult of these problems is linked to the fact that the designers of mechanical products have been trained carefully to understand the constraints, but now these constraints no longer exist. There is nothing more difficult, psychologically speaking, than giving up all the modes of thought which gifted teachers have carefully inculcated in one for years and which have then been applied carefully throughout one's career. It has often been said that it will be necessary for mechanical engineering experts to learn about microelectronics. I really do not think that is the main problem, although microelectronics is so important that understanding it today is now essential for scientists or technicians. A mechanical engineer can get by without knowing much in detail about the microelectronics products he uses. He can consider them as a kind of black box which produce a particular effect. That may suffice but, on the other hand, he is the person responsible for redesigning his product and must realize that the frontiers which confined his imagination no longer exist. If he does not venture beyond those borders, others will take this step. Our Japanese friends will probably be in a good position to do so. So much the better for them—but so much the worse for the European countries if they do not manage to do so at the right time. We must act at the right time.

There are, in addition, implications for the mechanical industries, for universities, whatever the higher education system involved, and for governments. It will require continuing education programmes which will be hard to achieve, since the people to be retrained are not underemployed. They do not have much free time, so it will be difficult to arrange further training.

Another problem stems from the fact that proper utilization of microelectronics in mechanical or electromechanical devices implies that all the required data for development are available. One must also have actuators adapted for the particular task to be carried out and they must be adapted for microelectronic controls, they must prove very reliable and be very cheap. Progress in microelectronics has been fast, but these actuators have not been developed as quickly as microelectronics demand. There is room for development which may have considerable consequences, which may require the proper use of electronics, yet which is very difficult to handle. It is difficult because it implies a combination of knowledge from research workers in the field who must also know about physics. After all, these actuators involve some physical measurement. It is difficult, because the variety of sensors and the factors involved is considerable and it is not clear whether the poorer manufacturers of such products in this field can make enough profit. Unfortunately, components, whether electronic or electromechanical, turn out to be at the very end of an industrial chain. They are very often the victims of price reductions and oscillations in the market. Once again, I am convinced that special efforts are required in enterprises of all kinds so we can solve the actuator and sensor problem and solve it in time, and in the context of ever-increasing worldwide competition.

Furthermore, the products designed will involve problems of use and after sales service. I am not very anxious about the problems of using such products. People have always underestimated the ability of consumers to adapt. I recall the time when automobiles were introduced: it was said they were a product for 'professional' drivers. People could not conceive that a user might drive his own car—only a chauffeur or a special sports driver would dare to drive one of these contraptions. How could the man in the street manage such a complex product? The truth is that virtually everyone now knows how to drive, even though dashboards have ever-increasing numbers of gadgets and buttons. Consequently, consumers will adapt to new products. Instead of turning a knob, they will have to strike a keyboard.

The idea of a mean time before failure of hundreds of thousands of hours could not have been thought of thirty or forty years ago. Today these performance levels are standard. Mechanical products, involve other parts aside from the electronic components, for instance the actuators and sensors to which I referred. It is possible to improve their reliability considerably but I do not think they can ever reach the 10^8 mtbf characteristic of electronics. In after sales service, the problems are even more complex. This work has to be carried out in the field. It is often hard to find people willing to do this work and it is also hard to monitor their work. How do you know whether the repair man spent five hours at the job as he claimed, or whether he did the job in two hours then went to see his girlfriend? These people will have to receive a thorough new kind of training.

There are possibilities for a revolution in the design of mechanical products that will create very difficult problems. I believe that developed countries, and countries such as Japan and those in Europe, which have in common a lack of raw materials for energy or minerals, must engage in increasing intellectual added value. I think these countries, in order to make such transformations, must engage in training and research dealing with actuators and sensors and they must do this more swiftly than at present.

11 Microcomputers in the Japanese consumer durables industry—status and prospects

Tadashi Sasaki, Senior Executive Director,
Sharp Corporation, Japan

I propose to discuss the application of microcomputers to consumer durables, and to outline some future trends.

The application of the first microcomputers in Japan, developed jointly by Japanese calculator manufacturers and Intel, was in office equipment, for example electronic calculators and data processing terminals. The use of microcomputers has now extended to most industries; in commerce, manufacturing, traffic management, communications, medical electronics, consumer products and domestic appliances.

The use of microcomputers in consumer products has been growing rapidly in Japan. Though a few of these are eight-bit microcomputers, most are four-bit devices on a single chip.

More than half the microwave ovens and video tape recorders now sold in Japan are equipped with a microcomputer, and from now on the proportion of these devices fitted with them will increase rapidly. But it is not only sophisticated items like these that incorporate microcomputers—minor domestic appliances in Japan such as rice cookers and cooking timers now also use them.

Why is it that the microcomputer is being used in every part of our daily lives? The first reason is that technology has enabled us to produce cheap but sophisticated microcomputers that can perform a huge range of functions. The second is that the sensors and actuators needed to increase the number of microcomputer applications are being developed slowly but steadily. A third reason is the diffusion of software and the development of more sophisticated computer languages, which have helped promote the wide use of the microcomputer.

From the point of view of demand, there is obviously a universal desire for more convenience, and greater safety and comfort—precisely the things the microcomputer can provide. In audio and visual products microcomputers are used for fine tuning, which is too awkward to do manually, and remote control units. In the

Table 1   Microcomputer applications

Household:	Traffic/Transportation:
Automobiles	Signal control
Home appliances	Traffic control
Calculators	Station management
Toys	Shipping/flight
Self-education	Others
Others	
	Measurement/Test/Monitor:
Commerce/Office:	Measuring equipment
Office calculators	Analyzer
Sales	Monitor
Inventory	Medical electronics
Word processing	Testing equipment
Retail accounting	Others
Banking/computer terminal	
Office equipment	Telecommunication:
Others	Wire communication
	Data communication
Data Processing:	Image display communication
General purpose computer	Wireless communication
Peripheral terminal calculators	Broadcast
Science & technology calculators	Others
Others	
	Other Areas:
	System management
Industry:	Others
Production machine equipment	
Machine control	
Process control	
Data roger	
Production management	
Others	

home they are mainly used for accurate control of domestic appliances.

Consumer products accounted for 82 per cent, by volume, of all microcomputers used in 1980, and 58 per cent in terms of value. The difference is caused by the fact that relatively cheap microcomputers are used in consumer products compared with other devices. One may also find that volume growth in consumer products is slower than in other areas, though it continues to grow.

There are a few examples of voice synthesis and recognition functions in domestic products at the moment, but these will increase rapidly and will be as common in the home of the future as the standard electric motors is today.

Table 2   Production volume of home appliances
microcomputer application rate and outlook

		Year				
Appliance		1977	1978	1979	1980	1982
VTR	Production volume (1000)	962	1559	2245	2837	4131
	Microcomputer applied unit (1000)	96	234	920	1560	3016
	%	10	15	41	55	73
Microwave oven	Production volume (1000)	1724	1857	1767	1577	1615
	Microcomputer applied unit (1000)	172	464	530	639	888
	%	10	25	30	40	55
Air conditioner	Production volume (1000)	2934	3864	5478	5100	5560
	Microcomputer applied unit (1000)	30	190	820	1275	1945
	%	1	5	15	25	35
Tuner	Production volume (1000)	2280	2680	2820	2950	3220
	Microcomputer applied unit (1000)		50	140	200	550
	%		2	5	8	17

Source: Report on Microcomputers, published by Japan's Electronic Industrial Promotion Association in March, 1980.

What does the future hold for electronics in the home? Firstly, there is a trend towards putting greater intelligence into computer controlled consumer products. The line width of today's large scale integrated circuit (LSI) is several microns. The very large scale integrated circuit (VLSI) which has a line width of less than one micron, will be developed in the near future. Here speed will be several times that of today's LSIs, and integration 100 times greater. In addition, three dimensional LSIs are now being studied.

VLSI technology will be applied to microcomputers, ROMs, RAMs, and in intelligent sensors, to produce inexpensive consumer products with more intelligence, ease of handling, small size and a range of functions. At the same time, the materials from which the device will be made will vary from just silicon to chemical compounds

Table 3   Microcomputer applications to present consumer products

Home appliance	Major functions of microcomputer utilized in home appliance
Microwave oven	Cooking time set Defrostation/cooking sequence sets such as proper temperature set Timer
Refrigerator	Temperature set and display Automatic defrostation
Air conditioner	Temperature/humidity set and display 3 minute pause
Kerosene heater	Temperature set and display Emergency display
Washing machine	Washing/rinse/dehydrating time set Washing sequence set and display
TV	Automatic channel selection and memory Programme set timer Remote control
Car radio	Automatic channel selection and memory Frequency display
Cassette deck	Automatic music selection Automatic repetition of selected music Tape amount
Open deck	Automatic search Tape speed deflection display
Record player	Automatic programme search Music selection and programming Automatic playing

Source: 1980s Electronic Industry Yearbook, published by Dempa Shinbun.

and amorphous semiconductors. Thanks to progress being made in the life sciences, 'living' sensors and the 'man-made brain' will no longer remain a futuristic dream.

Secondly, the integration of equipment will be an increasingly important trend. Housekeeping, home entertainment, information and security systems will all come under the control of micro-computers, thus a central home computer will be a major element in increasing our standard of living. For example, a home security system could be developed to prevent fires, gas leaks and even

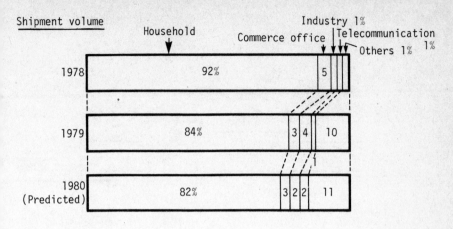

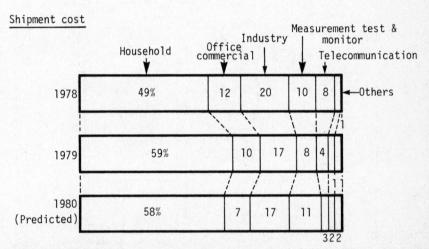

Figure 1   Microcomputer shipment rate by volume and cost.

burglaries by constantly monitoring the house and automatically reporting any danger. An energy saving system could also be developed to control and monitor the consumption of electricity, gas and water. Electricity costs would be reduced by using less energy at peak hours. Microcomputers are also likely to be the most efficient way of controlling and operating solar heating systems.

The microcomputer will have a major impact in the field of communications. Such services as viewdata (like the Captain system in Japan), electronic mail and home facsimile machines, will be of major significance, enabling a whole variety of software packages to be created. A housekeeping system, for example, could feature recipes, calorie counts and also control all the cooking equipment

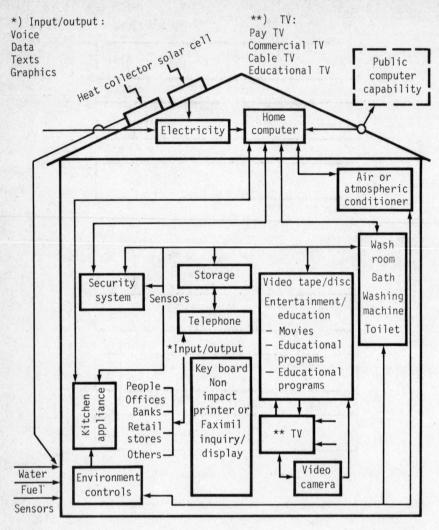

Figure 2   Future uses for home electronics systems.

in the kitchen. Paperwork such as budgeting, tax affairs and address books could be put on to the home computer. The computer will also play a part in leisure pursuits by providing games, or assisting with hobbies.

Thus everybody will have to be able to operate computers, and this will require its being made a much simpler process. Voice input and output are likely to be developed further—some products like clocks, calculators and automobiles already incorporate these factors

—and systems will be produced that guide the user to a much greater extent.

Advances in speech synthesis, and speaker-independent voice recognition systems, will drastically change the interface between man and machine. With such an interface, complicated equipment and systems could be handled by almost anybody.

At the same time there will be a constant movement from analogue to digital technology. This has already started to happen— television components have already been digitized thanks to VLSI —and PCM sound systems have been produced. Constantly falling costs will soon make digital systems very popular.

The transmission system will also be digitized in the future. By the year 2000 the analogue system will have been completely digitized in Japan, and we expect an international digital network to be established in the near future. To achieve this, wideband transmission lines must be used and here optical and satellite transmissions offer the best prospects. The development of these communications systems will be just as significant as the microcomputer itself. For example, if one had a computer and domestic facsimile unit, working full-time at home would be possible, and flexitime systems could be replaced by free time systems. Petrol used on business trips would also be cut to a minimum. With a communication system of this type, a chess enthusiast in Tokyo would be able to play chess with a colleague in Paris!

In conclusion, I would like to mention an important trend among industries involved in electronics. As the electronic technologies become integrated, so do the various parts of the industry—communications, data processing, office equipment, consumer products, electronic components etc. Prior to the 1960s, each industry had

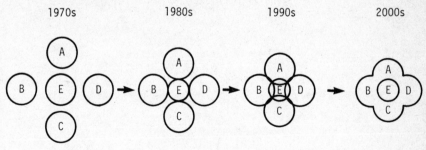

A: Data processing   B: Communication   C: Business equipment
        D: Consumer products   E: Components

Figure 3

conducted business on an independent basis. Recently, they have moved closer to one another and some have already been combined in certain areas. In the 1990s industry will become even more integrated and new industries will emerge that will not belong in any of the conventional groupings. All the industries based on electronics will draw closer and closer together making new products on a cooperative basis and these new products we hope may eventually create entirely new industries.

12 Telecommunications—innovation in the office
Rolf-Dieter Leinster, Consultant for the Chairman
of the Board of AEG-Telefunken AG, W. Germany

Some day, the 1980s may be described as the 'communic-eighties';
as a decade where the introduction of total communication fundamentally changed the quality and values of our lives.

WHAT IS TELECOMMUNICATIONS?

It is a long time from the invention of the telephone, telegraph, and
radio transmission to the development of the efficient communication systems of today. Thanks to technologies developed since the
1970s we are now entering an era of new dimensions and possibilities
in telecommunications. These include world-wide communication
networks based on satellite communications; the application of
the power of microelectronics in telecommunications equipment
and the merging of telecommunication and information technologies.
I have entitled this paper 'Telecommunication—innovation in the
office', because the office is the largest field of application for new
technologies related to information processing. It is here that wide
ranging changes in our organizations will originate.

WHAT IS THE IMPORTANCE OF INFORMATION?

Information processing will produce the differentiating potential in
the profile and the competitiveness of companies in the future.
A European study of manufacturing companies revealed average
information costs of 12 per cent of company revenue. I believe, however, that many companies are spending much more. In this context
banking and service industries dependent on the level of integration
of information processing serve as good examples.

The major part of today's information costs are in personnel
expenses, while only 10 per cent comprise hardware costs. This
explains why the office job is still cheapest in terms of investment
capital. In comparison, investment in production work amounts to

ten times, and in farming to fifteen times, that of investment in office equipment.

A further study has illustrated the inefficiency of office work by indicating that 90 per cent of white collar workers' time is spent in receiving information, 6 per cent in formulating results, and only 4 per cent in actual analytical and creative work. The same study concluded that, through an increase of investment in information technology in the office to $25000 per working place, from today's level of $3500, the present 4 per cent of time spent in creative work could be increased to 12 per cent, resulting in a fivefold productivity gain. It is also a fact that between 1960 and 1975 the increase in the number of office employees exceeded that of production workers by 100 per cent, and it is estimated that by the end of this century 75 per cent of the whole work force of the western industrialized countries will be employed in the administration and service sector, compared with 50 per cent today.

All this indicates that productivity will increase in two ways: not only by adopting information processing, but also by using such information in the intelligent way. In other words, emphasis must lie much more on the expansive multi-usage of information for generating decision power out of our information flow than on cost reduction in information gathering. Therefore the quality of tomorrow's information and communication infrastructures will become the most important company asset. The key assumption for our future strategy in this field is that we consider office work as a productive element.

WHAT ARE THE NEW OPPORTUNITIES?

How can and will this be achieved? Information processing in the office today is divided into different technical disciplines such as data processing, word processing and voice processing. Traditionally we have implemented all these separate elements of information processing as centralized concepts. This has resulted in segmenting the information process in separate and highly specialized functions. New telecommunication concepts will offer us communication systems where those elements are linked together into one system. This offers a new level of decentralization as multifunctional terminals will be able to offer a wide range of information for the user. The driving force behind this will be microelectronics. During the last decade the price–performance ratio in this field has shown a dramatic increase of a factor of 100 every ten years. Logic cost has decreased by 25 per cent each year and storage cost by 40 per cent every year.

We can expect that these developments will continue in the future. This assumption is based on the competitiveness of the industry, particularly because of Japan's work in this field and through the high research expenditure of the electronics industry. Spending 10 per cent of sales on R&D is not exceptional. In 1980, the twenty largest electronics companies in the USA invested 64 per cent of net profits in R&D. This amounted to 1.5×10^9.

Alternatively, the price–performance ratio in the telecommunications field, i.e. switching and transmission, will surpass that of the data processing industry. This will be triggered through new markets created by digitalization and wide-band information transport systems such as satellite and fibre optic communications and the creation of new PTT services.

Another important factor will be the availability of new technologies in a price range which allows decentralized applications such as speech and multifont character-recognition and new intelligent printers.

An important role will also be played by storage technologies in creating large data volumes such as discs based on laser technology, and associated storage equipment for extending decentralized information.

Although these functions for the end user will stimulate a growing decentralization, this does not mean that centralization will be totally absorbed. On the contrary, we will see a new centralization, the ability to communicate in a more universal way.

There is more than one way of achieving universal communication networks: there are in fact three different technological solutions. These are large central computers with hierarchical network architectures, digital programmable switching systems and intelligent local networks.

A further stimulating element will be the PTTs. Their large investments and R&D expenditures and the creation of new services like Teletex will encourage effective communication in the commercial and private fields. This technical progress can only be realized through close cooperation between producers, PTTs and users. This will guarantee the compatibility necessary to keep open all options for future technical innovation. Essential to this process is the establishment of international communication standards. Therefore, the primary decision in our companies will be the choice of the right communication infrastructure while the choice of hardware or even suppliers will become secondary.

In summary, information technology so far has been widely accepted because of the enormous hardware price improvements over the last decade. Merging this information technology with telecommunications will produce new attractive qualities for the design of future information processes. In order to appreciate the dimension of this quality change, the basic needs of the office have to be considered. I will concentrate on five major demands.

1 A reduction of the increasing amount of paper in our offices. I do not foresee at any time the paperless office. However, today already 25 per cent of all paper in offices is redundant. This means with new techniques we could decide to deal more directly and efficiently with information. Previous techniques have so far succeeded only in producing more paper.
2 The improvement of speech communication through more sophisticated hardware will grow in importance because speech communication will maintain a high content of the information processing function.
3 A significant improvement in the ratio of data recording and storage costs to the data utilization effects will become essential to increase the productivity of administrative workers and management who spend 80 per cent of their time dealing with information.
4 Information must not be segmented, but integrated. Different communication media must be interchangeable and compatible. This should lead to a technical information process more suited to human perception.
5 Information transport systems have to be created, permitting communication for everybody with anybody, everywhere and at all times.

In order to bridge the gap between these demands and technical capacity, we need a higher degree of application of today's technologies. We have innovation but lack intelligent technology applications. I see the four major areas for this innovation push as software technologies, user orientation, organization and management involvement.

The software shortage becomes evident in looking at programming productivity. While the speed of large central processors has improved by a factor of 100 over the last decade, programming productivity improved by a factor of only 12 during the same period. Consequently, software costs made up more than 60 per cent of the users' total data processing budget in 1980, compared with 30 per cent in 1975. Decentralization has increased this proportion as the amount of individual programming has grown. An improvement of programming productivity is essential.

More user-oriented applications are required for which standard applications are not an adequate answer. Information systems need to be attractive for the user, which means they must not force the users to think along fixed lines. Information systems have to adapt to the needs of the user. The quality of information systems therefore is not determined, as in the case of data-processing systems, by the quantity of information, but by the associative and imaginative combination of data. In other words the spontaneous and creative human nature which works on analogue principles and is not digitally oriented has to be reflected in the creation of suitable software.

WHAT STRUCTURAL AND MANAGEMENT CHANGES ARE NECESSARY?

We have seen that certain technical prerequisites have to be established, but I am certain this will not constitute a major problem. We cannot introduce new technologies into existing structures and organizations that are based on yesterday's technologies and thinking, otherwise our offices will become more expensive and less productive. This is why the information processing techniques of tomorrow require a fundamental change in our existing organization.

The traditional, centralized automation concept had its origin in the optimum utilization of equipment, which could not be provided with the broad variety of different tasks at the user level. Through the dramatic improvement of price performance ratios this is no longer a barrier to enforcing decentralization. Furthermore, the quality of content of decentralization supported by telecommunication allows us to design a workplace more adapted to human needs. This will improve motivation and, as a result, lead to improved productivity. It will develop a new consciousness at the user level. The user could be involved in the definition and design of the workplace and this will be a major incentive for the increased penetration of new techniques. I believe it is important that employees should be able to determine their immediate working environment. The realization of this new consciousness will certainly require a larger investment per workplace in human capital terms than the investment in hardware.

Another aspect related to organization is that new communicative technologies are not warmly welcomed in traditional, hierarchical, organizational structures, because new technologies offer a much higher degree of flexibility. However, this is precisely the attractive potential of new technologies. In the area of management the obvious gap between technological innovation and existing management techniques has to be closed.

Information processing has not only grown in complexity but also in its scope of application. What we do need more of in the future is a technically competent function for managing company-wide information systems based on the integration of information technologies and telecommunications, thereby guaranteeing the compatibility of communication networks in the future. For managing the cost of information processing and its profit potential, an information controller, as suggested by Diebold, could enable information processing to yield more tangible results.

One of the reasons for the relatively small penetration of information technologies in the office is the low level of professionalism in cost justifying office work. Furthermore, with the growing availability of a choice of different communication media and PTT services, cost optimization becomes a management task. Last, but not least, the improved functions of information technologies enhance their relevance to top management, not only because of their importance for the internal information processing, but also in their external use. I believe we will see not only the possible transfer of some of today's office work into the private households of employees, but the integration of new techniques into the products and services of our companies: for example, the maintenance systems for electronic products could be operated by using computerized diagnosis systems through telecommunications. This illustrates the growing strategic importance of information handling in companies.

WHAT ARE EUROPE'S CHANCES?

Information plays a vital role in companies and has quantitative dimensions such as the biggest cost factor and largest cost reduction potential; and a qualitative dimension which is its untapped potential. The application of telecommunications in our offices will enable us not only to manage that valuable resource called information more efficiently, but also to take account of the needs and desires of employees; thus bridging two so far irreconcilable positions, that of rationalization and job satisfaction: creating the motivation in our companies that is necessary to achieve higher productivity.

This process will not only produce dramatic changes within company structures, but will also induce a metamorphosis in the whole industry. In the marketing of information systems a reshuffling of established structures and responsibilities will occur. This metamorphosis will not only affect single companies and industries, but will lead to a reshaping of whole industrial structures and positions. I believe that in this new equilibrium between technological, industrial and market powers Europe could take a much stronger position than the one it holds today.

I see five basic strengths for the European market-place:

Systems know-how

Europe, and especially France, the UK, Germany, Switzerland, and the Scandinavian countries are among the most advanced users in the world of information technology. This has established a vast reservoir of systems knowledge in Europe. Inasmuch as the growing demand for cost reductions has transformed the development and manufacturing of information equipment into a black box business, so systems knowledge will be important in future marketing— particularly as the users of complex telecommunication systems need a systems integrator.

Software capabilities

Based on the sophisticated European user environment, software resources are built up which could give Europe a lead in software technology not only in the field of commercial applications but also in the area of an extended deployment of microcomputers in industrial products and in VLSI design.

Telecommunications know-how

The European telecommunications industry is recognized as technologically innovative. Its close relations with the national PTTs and their progressive activities in the area of new services such as teletex and viewdata will create new markets for better and cheaper user-oriented products, despite well established PTT monopolies.

Government initiatives

The strong interest which some European governments have taken in programmes concerning telecommunications and information technologies should lead to the enhancement of the industry's strength. These programmes will be oriented towards new methods, particularly in the field of software and machine tools. Government initiatives should not question the role of industry to compete on an international basis. This includes not only the global marketability of new products, but also the need for international joint ventures with major market powers like Japan and the USA.

Experience with codetermination

The cooperation with tariff partners within the advanced structure of codetermination in Europe, and especially in Germany, is strongly influencing equipment design in areas like ergonomics. From my experience with codetermination I believe unions are not against the introduction of new technologies on principle. They are, however, extremely concerned about the lack of employee involvement in the design of the working environment and also the management of change with regard to the qualifications of workers which has to be accomplished as a result of the emergence of new technologies.

I have tried to describe the possibilities for innovation in Europe in the field of telecommunications and information. There is, however, no ideal formula for making use of these chances. The results will depend on the amount of dedication put into our efforts in Europe.

Let me close with a quotation from the report by Simon Nora and Alain Minc entitled: *L'Information de la Societé.*

The new challenge is uncertainty. There are no sure predictions, but only right questions on the ways and means to be taken for reaching the desired goals. The future cannot be based on predictions but on objectives and plans and the capability to give oneself the suitable organizations for a realization of the future.

13   The office automation industry—status and prospects

Kohei Amou, General Manager, Industrial Electronics
Planning Department, Shibaura Electronic Company Ltd.
(Toshiba), Tokyo, Japan

Prior to the 1970s production efficiency was mainly related to the
rationalization of manufacturing. In the 1980s, however, it is becoming widely recognized that labour costs incurred in office routines
continue to increase even though the latest equipment is used. The
result is a demand for the streamlining of office operations with
more efficient equipment, namely, office automation (OA). Manufacturing is based on machinery, but the office is organized around
human labour. The equipment designed for improved office efficiency
is, therefore, aimed at supporting rather than replacing office personnel. Ergonomically designed, easy to operate office equipment is
of supreme importance in promoting OA, and because of this the
trend has been to create more intelligent equipment by using microprocessors. These, together with memory and display devices, are
rapidly being incorporated into present day OA equipment. Microprocessors will play a vital role in streamlining office routines and
may play as important, if not more so, a part as electronics played in
manufacturing rationalization.

Table 1 shows that USA investment in manufacturing equipment
was brisk from 1968 to 1978, with a 90 per cent increase in productivity. Investment in offices, however, was low with an improved
productivity of only 4 per cent, although the people involved
accounted for nearly 50 per cent of the total working population.
In Japan, office workers are projected to increase from 18 million
(38 per cent of the total working population) in 1970, to an estimated 25 million (45 per cent) in 1985 (see Table 2). The number
of people engaged in manufacturing, however, will remain unchanged
at around 15 million, and there will be a decrease in percentage
terms from 32 per cent in 1970, to 28 per cent in 1985.

The increase in labour costs between manufacturing and office
work from 1967 to 1977 is compared in Figure 1. The comparison,
based on a survey conducted in the major organizations listed with
the Tokyo Stock Exchange, shows the ratio of labour costs to total

Table 1 Office vs. manufacturing investment in USA

	Manufacturing	*Offices*
1. Facility investment per person	¥5000000 ($25000)	¥400000 ($2000)
Increase in productivity for ten years	90%	4%
2. Office workers as percentage of employees (Rate of office cost)		50% (about 30%→ 40%∿50%) (Exchange rate $1 = ¥200)

Source: SIR: 1968–1971.

Table 2 Change in number of office workers in Japan (millions)

	1970	*1975*	*1985**
Total number of workers	(100) 47 (100%)	(107) 51 (100%)	(118) 56 (100%)
Total number of office workers	(100) 18 (38%)	(117) 21 (41%)	(138) 25 (45%)
Total number of production workers	(100) 15 (32%)	(100) 15 (29%)	(105) 16 (28%)

(A Labour White Paper 1979, * Estimated.)

sales. The labour costs in manufacturing, even with a decrease in some enterprises, show an overall increase. The cost for those in office work shows an increase of 90 per cent. The 45° line indicates an equal increase between manufacturing and office labour costs. Excepting the automobile industry, office labour costs tend to increase in ratio to the sales total.

To what extent is productivity improved when office operations are streamlined? Table 3 is an estimate made of Japan's GNP from 1980 to 1990 and shows the need for productivity to be improved

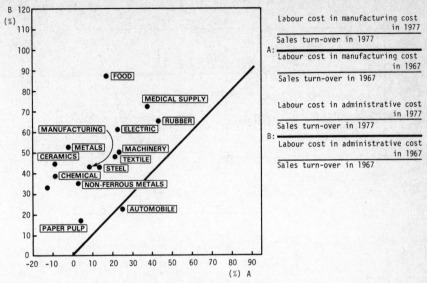

Figure 1   Comparisons between blue and white collar labour costs.

at annual rate of 5.5 per cent to accommodate a 0.7 per cent increase per annum. If office workers continue to account for nearly 50 per cent of the total, then this provides the numerical requirement for streamlining office routine.

Looking at the equipment used in offices from the viewpoint of the office automation industry, OA products can be broadly divided into three groups: business machines; communication systems; and data processing systems. Figure 2 shows the production scales for major OA equipment, and all the product categories indicated show

Table 3   Estimated economic growth in Japan

	1980	1990
GNP	¥247 trillion ($1.23 trillion)*	¥693 trillion ($2.46 trillion)*
Nominal	2.8 times	
Real	1.8 times	
Growth rate (per year)	6.2% (real)	
Increase in labour force (per year)	0.7%	
Increase in productivity (per year)	5.5%	

(*Exchange rate $1 = ¥200)
(Estimated by Economic Planning Agency)

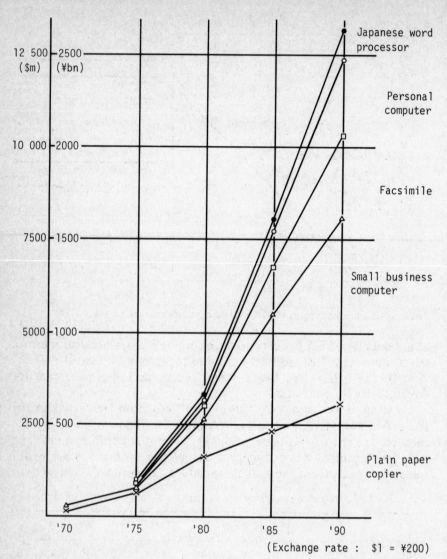

Figure 2   Production of major office automation equipment. *Source*: Japan Office Equipment Association.

an expanding market. Together, these markets are expected to grow at an average annual rate of 15 per cent, becoming a ¥1 trillion ($5 billion) industry in 1982.

The number of Japanese OA manufacturers and their export ratios is shown in Table 4. The number of companies is still increasing, and the rapid development of microprocessors, together

Table 4   Number of Japanese OA equipment manufacturers
and their export rates

	PPC	*SBC*	*FAX*	*PC*	*WP*
Number of manufacturers	16	70	21	30	19
Export rate in 1980 (%)	66	3.4	19	15	0

with their cost reduction, has accelerated the proliferation of OA
equipment.

Figure 3 gives a summary of the types of jobs being done by
manual labour in offices. The two main office routines can be
broadly classified into communication and documentation. As shown

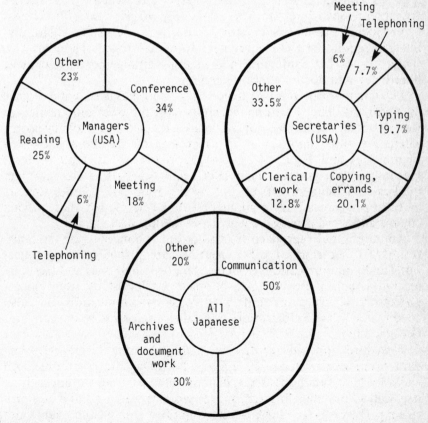

Figure 3   Breakdown of office functions—USA and Japan.

in Figure 3, the job content in the USA varies according to each staff level. Managers or controllers, in particular, undertake less writing or typing. For Japan the average is indicated, because detailed surveys are not available; but generally, seniors tend to engage in communication, while juniors are involved in documentation or word processing. Communication includes conversation and arrangements, meetings or conferences, and document dispatch. Documentation includes document preparation, and document rearrangement, distribution, and duplication.

In the communication category, conversation and arrangements are concerned with a human element that cannot be replaced by a machine. There is, however, equipment that can support people in this function. One example is daily schedule control—particularly involving enquiries, arrangements, or conference and reception room reservations, performed by people using telephones. This requires considerable labour time, especially when other parties are out or when lines are busy; thus only 30 per cent effectiveness is considered possible. Such work could be performed mechanically, but will require new OA equipment to be developed. There are also similar needs for conference and meeting arrangements, document dispatches, and documentation handling.

The summary of the two major office routines is shown in Figure 4(a) and (b). The electronic secretary and the electronic mailer, as we call them, act in place of a human secretary and mail envelopes. There are three approaches in executing the functions shown in Figure 4(a) and Figure 4(b). One approach is based on business machines. Plain paper copiers (PPC) and typewriters are the main business machines in offices and by incorporating microprocessors in these machines, OA equipment can be developed that provide copiers and word processors with more intelligence.

An alternative approach is based on communication systems. About 50 per cent of office routines are linked to communications and communications systems, such as telephones and facsimile machines, and these can also be made intelligent by using microprocessors which allow not only voice communication, but also coded and image information transmissions for incorporation into OA equipment.

The third approach centres on data processing systems. On-line data processing systems are equipped with a data communication and data base functions. Thus, man machine communication technology can add intelligent functions for word processing and image processing. The progress of OA is following three parallel approaches and these become integrated as the intelligence of equipment increases.

(a) Communication

Work	OA device, its function
1 Conversation, consultation (very human activities)	
Schedule control (inquiry and appointment)	Electronic secretary
Reservation of reception room	Electronic secretary
Remote conversation through multi-function telephone	
2 Conference	Electronic secretary
Scheduling, notice and reservation	
Telephone conference, TV conference	
Preparation and demonstration	
Preparation of minutes of materials	
3 Dispatch	Electronic mailing
Memorizing documents and figures, dispatch and receipt	

(b) Document processing

Work	OA device, its function
1 Documentation	
Preparing documents in Chinese characters and Kana characters by key-board, OCR and speech input	JWP
Memorizing, transaction, correcting and editing of a specimen document	JWP
Preparing documents with figures, graphing and picturing data	
Printing	
2 Paper arrangement	
Easy transaction filing	Data-base, picture-file
Document distribution	Electronic mailing
Partial copy, duplicated copy, editing copy	Intelligent copier

Figure 4   Elements of office work.

As shown in Figure 5, OA systems are based on business machines (B), communication systems (C), and data processing systems (D). The basic equipment will be combined to develop new products, which will integrate further to improve OA. The key to implementing this process is the technology for making equipment intelligent, compact, and cheap by using electronic devices based on microprocessors.

The first level of Figure 5 represents the existing equipment. The second level is the equipment that is made intelligent for easier operation or combined functions. The third level is the equipment that is integrated into a system based on the developments made in the stages up to the second level. The present stage sees the advent of combined equipment for OA. Thus OA is the process of equipment (B), (C), and (D) being made intelligent by using microprocessors, then combined and united into high-efficiency systems.

The equipment (B), (C), and (D) on the first level is now in regular use. Business machines (B) and communication systems (C), however, do not incorporate microprocessors because (B) and (C) were produced before mircoprocessors came into use. Data processing systems (D) use microprocessors that play a vital role and form the nucleus of terminals as the controllers. The equipment and systems on the second level are now on the market or will be available in the near future. None of these could be achieved without microprocessors.

A personal computer is the product of microprocessor technology and an OA system using local area networks. Personal computers have rapidly widened their office application range since their initial hobby stage, thanks to the progress in LSI technology, which has led to low-priced computers. The Toshiba personal computer, Pasopia, is standardized with an 8-bit microprocessor equipped with 64 K bytes of RAM (random access memory). A wide variety of optional devices is available, including floppy disks, colour CRT (cathode ray tubes) displays, LCD (liquid crystal displays), dot printers and audio cassette tapes, as shown in Figure 6. With these options there is a choice of components available for systems in the same way that an audio enthusiast has various options when selecting audio equipment. Rapid progress has been made to include highly enhanced functions with the advent of personal computers incorporating a 16-bit microprocessor.

Office automation systems are regarded as the final stage in OA. These service and supporting functions have not reached the full level of acceptance in our society, however, developments have already been made on the basic system configuration, such as the

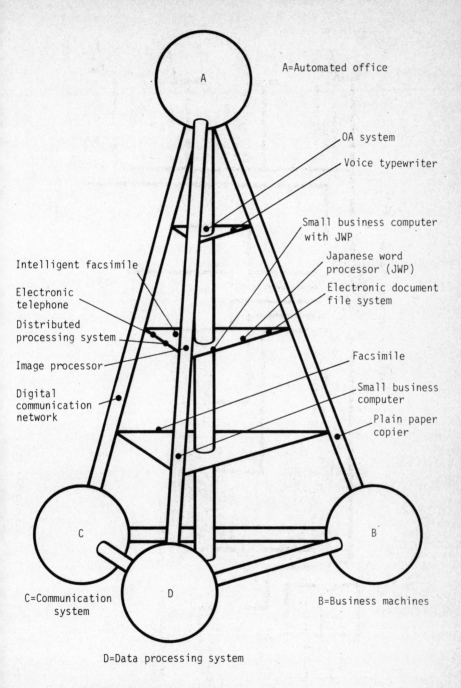

Figure 5   The office automation concept.

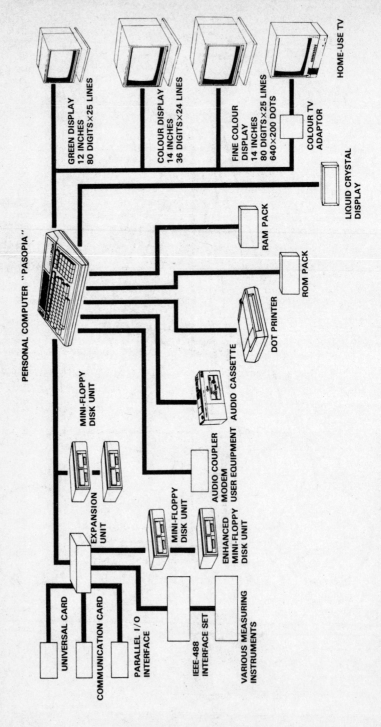

Figure 6   The Toshiba personal computer PASOPIA system.

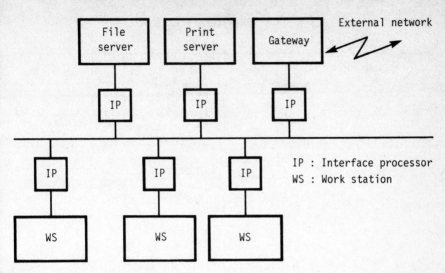

Figure 7   Xerox ETHERNET system.

Xerox Ethernet system. As shown in Figure 7, the system is based on the local area network with intelligent work stations located in various places in an office. Through the local area network, these work stations are connected to the file server that supports the data base, as well as the print server for printouts. The local area network is also connected to external computer networks for communication with distant offices through the work stations.

About 70 per cent of the information occurring in one office is usually used internally, with limited information being communicated between external offices. This example uses a high-speed network as an exclusive local area network to maximize processing efficiency, which means the system matches perfectly the form of office work routines.

Xerox has also announced the development of an LSI microprocessor for exclusive use as an interface to the Ethernet for execution of the basic transmission procedure. So far, its work station, file server and print server execute comparatively limited functions. The Ethernet OA system is a distributed data processing type that performs particular office routines and therefore will be widely accepted as its software becomes consolidated.

There are three major differences in the forms of office routines when comparing Japanese and Western countries. One of these differences is of course language. Western countries have a long history of alphabetical typewriters, which facilitate documentation when using a word processor. In Japan, there are more than 3000

Table 5   Differences in types of office work in Japan and
Western countries

	Western countries	Japan
1	Alphabets Word processors	Chinese characters Handwritten manuscripts (facsimile) OCR by Chinese character Speech recognition
2	Division of work Specialization (contract basis)	Uniformity Jobs performable by anyone (group-oriented)
3	Top-down procedure Preparation of documents by dictation Spoken language	Bottom-up procedure Circulating paper for consensus Literary language

characters (including Chinese characters) in daily use. In this context the potential distribution of Japanese word processors is massive as at present the majority of office workers have to *write* these characters for documentation purposes. In the future, information inputs using Kanji optical character recognition and voice recognition are expected. Voice recognition is much more applicable to the Japanese language, which consists of fewer syllables than Western language.

Another difference involves social structure. Japanese society is quite homogeneous, with limited differentiation of occupations. In Japan, one job is performed by a group of people and for cultural reasons the concept of contracts is not strong. The reverse of these situations is generally true in Western countries.

A further difference in Western countries is that the decision-making function tends to be determined by managers in a hierarchical manner. In Japan initiatives are often taken by juniors.

A further character of Western nations is that their documentation uses oral recordings because there is little difference between the written and spoken word. In Japan, written documentation is also necessary because of the Japanese system of consensus formation, which involves circulating documentation or drafts of plans for executive approval.

The methods of performing office work are peculiar to the respective socities. Therefore, office staff working in different social environments require the support of varying types of OA systems to perform their duties more efficiently. In order to develop the software to make OA systems both useful and productive, it is necessary for individual countries to incorporate the characteristics inherent in their societies.

14 Microelectronics—threat or opportunity?
Albert Jan Huart, Managing Director,
Semiconductor Operation,
NV Philips, Holland

Many people see microelectronics as a threat to their way of life. There are frequent confrontations with microelectronics at work, but one can also find many applications of microelectronics in the home which would be greatly missed if they were suddenly taken away. Let us look at the issue from a different viewpoint, that of the manufacturer. The producers of devices in the microelectronics field must find markets and applications for their products. They must proclaim the virtues of microelectronics and the opportunities it offers us all now and tomorrow. But this message will fall on deaf ears if the listener feels his job is threatened, by, for example, increasing automation. In fact, a large group of people now see microelectronics as a threat to the very existence of their jobs.

Today these people meet microelectronics at every turn: electronic alarms wake them from their beds, electronics bring them the morning news, they find it in their automobiles—controlling the ignition, calculating fuel consumption and the distance of the journey and providing them with music. They love it! But, when they arrive at work, they find microelectronics in charge of everything. The secretary's word processor, the designer's computer aids, factory production, testing, stock control, distribution, transportation—everything!

Do these same people grumble that their new systems do not work or that they are too expensive? Perhaps not. They understand the merits of increased outputs and efficiency as a result of microelectronics, so what then is the problem?

The problem is that the workforce feel they are no longer able to use their own creativity or initiative. They feel stifled by new developments which have taken away something of their freedom. It leads them to believe that microelectronics is a threat to their way of life and the reason for this fear is that change is being imposed upon them by those who control their working environment. Microelectronics for them implies change and uncertainty.

The advocates of this change are not usually members of that part of society affected by change. Thus, we find resistance being generated to counter the threat. On the other hand, in an affluent society new requirements and needs are emerging continuously. In many cases, these needs can be satisfied by microelectronics—to put it another way, there is a wide disparity between the technological capabilities of microelectronics and its acceptance by society.

I have already said the principal reason for many people rejecting microelectronics was based on the notion that it destroys their freedom and creativity at work. This view, however, is by no means shared by all. There are many activities at work in which microelectronics plays an important role by enhancing creativity—computer-aided design is but one example.

I have also mentioned some of the great advances in electronics which have improved our daily lives. Remember the picture of the dog listening to his master's voice? Today, we have Hi-Fi: tomorrow the quality of music will have improved by another order of magnitude (I refer here to the Audio Compact Disc concept).

Television has brought entertainment and visual information to the home and an awareness of the world at large, its cultures and customs. It brings laughter and tears, depicts conflicts—power and poverty, rich and poor. It takes us instantly into the heart of every occasion and in 'real time'. In the home, electronics can offer untold opportunities for stimulating creativity. I am not talking about TV games, which have been with us for a few years, but about applications of a perhaps more useful nature—for example the interactive TV set.

Microelectronics, particularly as a communication and information medium, offers us immense opportunities. It provides society with a chance to overcome some of the problems that surround it and to improve opportunities for the future.

There will be an enormous growth in electronic methods of communication during the next decade. Many of the tasks now performed of necessity at our offices and factories will be able to be carried out equally successfully at home. We are now witnessing a gradual transformation of our offices into communication centres. Even now, more than half of all clerical functions could be carried out away from the office, provided the same, or better, communication exists between management and staff. One would still dictate letters to a secretary and receive a printed copy, but she would be at home, maybe on the other side of the city!

Progress can be divided into three phases. The first of these was the time for gaining experience of new functions; an era in which mechanical tasks began to be replaced by electronics. Hard wired systems became integrated and all new functions became electronic. This phase is now over. The second phase is an era in which human intelligence can be conserved, where electronic communication will enable access and interaction with such intelligence, where automation will replace boring and repetitive human toil. This is a period of observation. We are looking at new forms of energy conservation, new possibilities for education and health care and novel forms of traffic control, as the highways of the world become more crowded. All these different areas have information as the common denominator. We should also examine the ability of society to accept a new concept for a future way of life.

The third phase is the period of interaction between clusters of information in different segments of society, an era in which cybernetics will eventually replace the fixed order—whether it is the subject of understanding between nations, between government and industry, or the compatibility of electronic systems; or whether we should consider the social interface for the communications function, by which knowledge is transferred world-wide, taking into account different cultures. Here, I see the greatest problems and the greatest opportunities. I believe these problems have one common factor, namely that they are interface problems.

In principle, the solution to these problems is simple and lies in standardization. However, implementation is very difficult. The issue is always the same, the problems of coordination, definition and development of the necessary standards. In many cases, we do not even know who to consult. The electronics industry has a tendency to keep developing and producing in a particular field, with the result that, when it comes to discussions with other branches of industry, or social or political organizations, it is already too late. The answer is in our hands. We must pool our ideas and cooperate. We must also stand above dogmatism and personal and national prejudice. We must listen without bias.

An important category of problems is formed by the fact that most electronic equipment not only has to fit into existing systems, but also into systems not yet developed. Let me give you an example. In the home, we are confronted with a variety of equipment, all of which has to be connected—radio, television, Hi-Fi, video machines, etc. There are numerous brands of each type of equipment and the user must be able to dictate the way it all connects. Philips has invented a bus system for doing this—the Domestic Digital Bus, which enables any unit with the proper interface to connect with the bus. Here every unit joined to the bus can communicate with any other without difficulty and without the user requiring any technical knowledge. We have defined the interface. But, we have gone further —to enable integrated circuits and functional modules to connect within the equipment, Philips has invented another bus—the Inter IC Bus. It enables all microprocessors and associated circuits connected to the bus to communicate with each other in a straightforward manner. Yet another example is the VME Bus, an attempt to standardize interconnections for 16- and 32-bit microcomputer systems.

I have already mentioned the social interface for communication. Interfaces do not function adequately without defined standards, and communication and language are two sides of the same coin. In the final analysis, interfaces and the underlying standards constitute a language problem. In technical standardization, language stays in the background but becomes more apparent when a need to communicate between society and industry arises. For that interface, another language is required, a language which appeals to the user and we in industry still have to learn to speak that language. We must act to set standards—for interface, communications and so on. We must think in terms of a world where electronic data processing will be a hardware configuration, surrounded by universally acceptable software. We must develop a simple world language for communication. Developments in electronic methods of communication are happening with astonishing speed. It is not the rate of progress that troubles me so much as the direction it is taking. I repeat, we must pool our ideas and we must cooperate. We must work together to achieve standardization, universally acceptable inputs and a simple common language. If we do not, if we continue to pursue individual goals, then proliferation will increase and chaos can be the only outcome.

If Japan braces herself to cope with the microelectronics future of Japanese society, we should all study and discuss the proposals. But, if Japan's goal is domination of the world markets, disaster will result. This also applies to Europe and the USA. If one community or country tries to dominate this vast and very important field, there will be chaos.

As a medium for communication, electronics can provide a simple way to disseminate large volumes of information around the world. The value is, as such, indeterminate. What gives it value is the degree of reception—we must give it meaning. I believe we will see a change in our society from what could be called a technically-oriented people to more artistic, craft-oriented, playful people. Since microelectronics is approaching the level of human thought processes, it may well stimulate creativity in return.

In this context, let me quote the words of Jean-Jacques Servan-Schreiber. He said 'The very nature of the computerized society rests on the full employment of every person's abilities. The more it is adapted to individuality, the more it accelerates the process of new creativity which, in turn, will demand greater human input and thought.'

Only human beings possess the ability to reason—no computer, no matter how clever, can do better than man himself. But, we must learn to use the medium appropriately and give it meaning for mankind. We must increase efforts in this direction. Today, we are laying the foundations of the future. If we observe the safeguards I have mentioned, if we pool our ideas and cooperate, then microelectronics can offer unprecedented opportunities for a better life. Microelectronics provides a means of communication between peoples of all colours, creeds and cultures throughout the world on an individual basis, in an interactive world where interfaces are defined, rather than using the fixed presumptions of the present. This will be an era in which flexibility and adaptability will prevail over rigidity and dogmatism, where cybernetics will replace the fixed order. This is the third phase which I referred to earlier—the Wienerian world. We must ensure microelectronics does not become a threat to industry or society; we must pool ideas and cooperate. I firmly believe microelectronics offers us a great chance for our future and the future of our children.

15 The microcomputer revolution in Japanese society
Yoichi Tao, President, Institute of Researching
Life Structures, Japan

Volume (1 000)

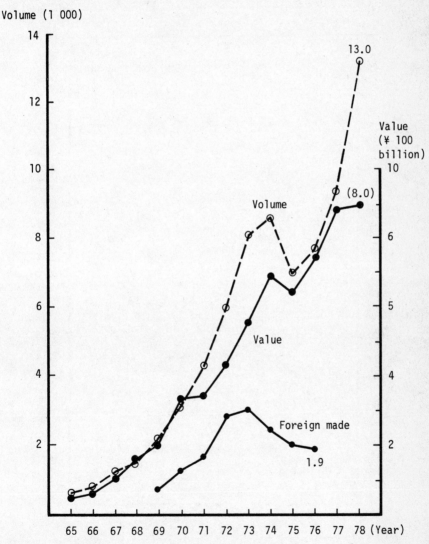

Figure 1 General purpose computer: shipment trends.

THE PERSONAL COMPUTER INDUSTRY

Trends in manufacturing

Shipments of general purpose computers

Japanese manufacturers started making general purpose computers in 1957, and by 1964 computers had become a major industry, thanks to the rapid development of technology and constant research and development. By 1969 more than half the computers sold in Japan were made there.

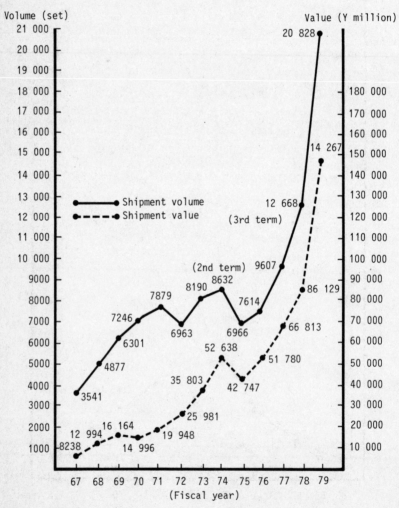

Figure 2   Shipment volume and value trends of office computers.

Shipments of office computers

Office computers are those costing less than $150000 each, which are used to automate ordinary office work. Sales of these have grown rapidly and in 1979 $700 million worth were sold.

Figure 3   Export and import value of computers (main body and peripheral equipment).

Import and export trends of computers and peripheral equipment

Despite the rapid growth in Japan's domestic computer production, imports of computers and peripheral equipment still exceed exports, although the trade gap has narrowed considerably since 1975.

Development of the personal computer market in Japan

As with other types of computer, personal computers were initially imported into Japan from the USA. Since then, domestic production has gradually begun to catch up. The first period of imports was based on Intel's SDK–80 and the KIM–1 from MCS, both single board computers imported from the USA. A year later NEC started production of an equivalent, the TK–80, and Toshiba followed with the EX–80. In 1978 more sophisticated American computers arrived in the form of the Apple II, the PET, and the TRS–80. In the following year, Sharp brought out the MZ–80 and NEC produced its PC–8001.

By 1980, about twenty Japanese manufacturers were making 25 types of personal computer, with almost as many foreign competitors. Overall sales increased from 30000 units in 1979 to 110000

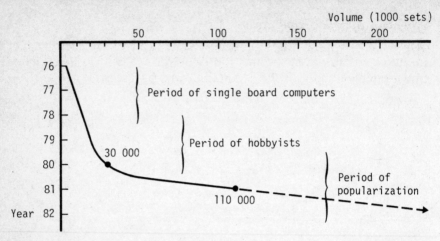

Figure 4   History of personal computers in Japan.

in 1980, worth $165 million. There are now an estimated 150000 personal computers in Japan.

Personal computers—shares between industries

At the end of 1980, Japanese manufacturers dominated more than 90 per cent of the personal computer market. If the period until 1980 is known as the hobbyist period, 1981 should be called the year when personal computers began to be used for practical purposes. At the Data Show in October of that year, several new types of device were displayed.

General purpose computers have dominated the market and there are about fifty manufacturers computing to sell about seventy different types of device. Basic and Pascal are the two most popular languages used for these computers, although other languages can be used with some of the machines.

NEC: PC-8001

NEC's PC-8001 personal computer has the largest single share of the Japanese market. The main body costs $840, it has 24 K byte of ROM (read only memory), which can be increased to 32 K byte, and 16 K byte of RAM (random access memory), which can be expanded to 32 K byte. It can be used with a variety of input and output devices. With a 12-inch colour display, it gives 80 letters per line, 160 × 100 dots of analytic capacity, and eight possible colours.

NEC has announced a new computer, the 6000, costing $449 for the main body; and with the colour display, printer and data recorder, $1183. It also has its 8800 series, which has a 185 byte

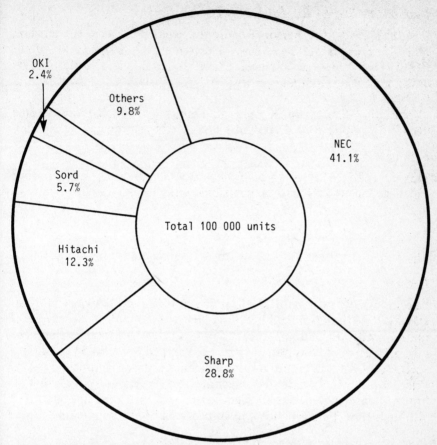

Figure 5   Volume of personal computers produced in Japan (1980); breakdown by manufacturers.

memory, the ability to compose Japanese sentences, and high quality graphics resolution (640 × 400 dots).

Sharp MZ–80B

This unit holds the second largest share of the Japanese personal computer market and is typical of Sharp's range. With four K byte of ROM and 64 K byte of RAM, a green ten-inch CRT display and cassette storage, it costs $1390. Hardware options include floppy disk drive, a dot-printer and a 14-inch colour display.

Hitachi: Basic Master Level III

This costs $1490 for the main body and has 24 K byte of ROM and 32 K byte of RAM.

Toshiba: PASOPIA BP-100

Toshiba's PASOPIA personal computer went on sale in the autumn of 1981. It costs $800 and has 64 K byte of RAM and 32 K byte of ROM. Two types of Japanese characters, Kanji and Kana, can be used, and it is compatible with a large variety of hardware and software.

The BP-100 has 48 K byte of memory, a 9-inch monochrome display, a floppy disk drive and a dot matrix printer. It costs $1550.

Fujitsu: FM 8

This costs $1090, has 64 K byte of RAM and ROM, can produce Japanese characters and is available with a high quality graphics display.

Peripheral equipment manufacturers

There are more than 300 makers of peripheral equipment in Japan.

Future of the personal computer market

Sales for 1981 will be 300000 units, doubling to between 600000 and 700000 units in 1982. Shipments in 1981 will be worth $500 million, with $1 billion forecast for 1982. By 1983, more than one million personal computers will be shipped, worth $1.5 billion, accounting for one third of the general purpose computer market. Prices of hobbyist oriented machines and portable units will fall, but systems aimed at business users will not become cheaper, although their performance will improve as the price remains stable.

Future computers with greater sophistication

Better hardware performance and increased memory are bound to occur and colour graphics, Japanese language processing, voice recognition and networking will all develop rapidly.

The software industry

Net sales turnover in the informatics industry

Figure 8 shows the annual turnover in computer services, including software development, data processing, and information supply services. Since it is based on 1978 statistics, data for personal computers are essentially excluded. In 1978, the turnover had already risen to nearly $2.5 billion, and this increase will continue.

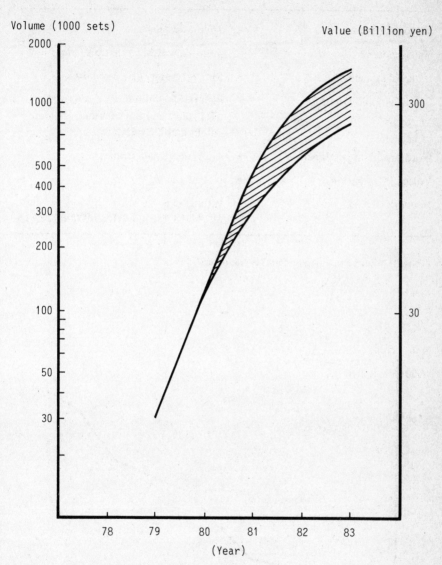

Figure 6   Shipment trends of personal computers in Japan: past records and market forecasts.

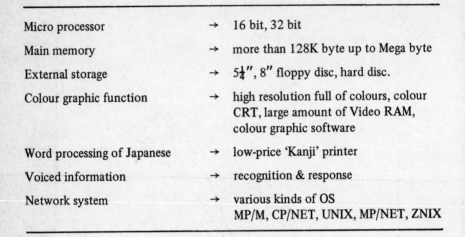

Micro processor	→	16 bit, 32 bit
Main memory	→	more than 128K byte up to Mega byte
External storage	→	5¼", 8" floppy disc, hard disc.
Colour graphic function	→	high resolution full of colours, colour CRT, large amount of Video RAM, colour graphic software
Word processing of Japanese	→	low-price 'Kanji' printer
Voiced information	→	recognition & response
Network system	→	various kinds of OS MP/M, CP/NET, UNIX, MP/NET, ZNIX

Figure 7   Future function of personal computers.

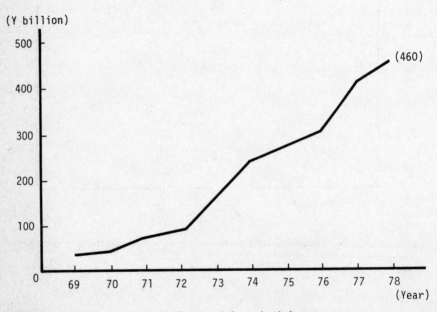

Figure 8   Trends in turnover in the Japanese information industry.

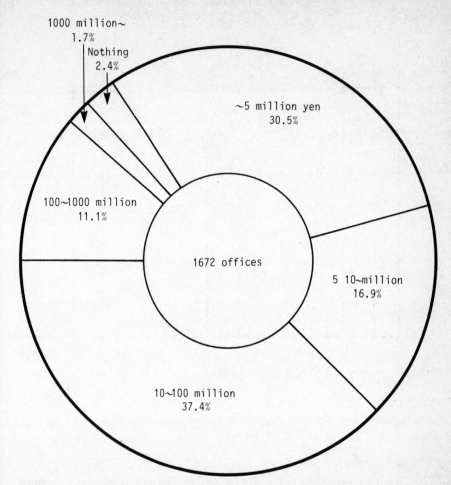

Figure 9 Breakdown of offices by capital base scales: 1978 information processing industry.

Breakdown of companies

In 1978 there were 1672 companies in the information service industry, but half of them were small, having assets below $50000. Such innovative, small companies will grow in number as personal computers become more common.

Trends in data processing employment

According to the 1980 National Census, based on a one per cent sample, about 130000 men and women work as data processing experts. The number of female employees has been growing as fast as

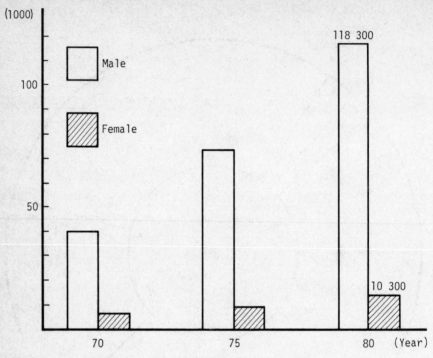

Figure 10   Rate of increase in information processing experts (National Census).

the number of male workers. Employees of this type are not spread out equally throughout Japan, however, and the total number will exceed that shown in Figure 10.

The newly developed packaged software

The amount of available software for personal computers has been increasing rapidly. The amount of software bought by companies to do their order processing has not been revealed, but with the arrival of personal computers, several thousand orders have been placed for complete software packages.

Figure 11 shows how 700 software packages have been used by owners of NEC's PC-8000 personal computer. As software becomes increasingly important, the Japanese domestic market will demand the basic software that best suits Japanese applications.

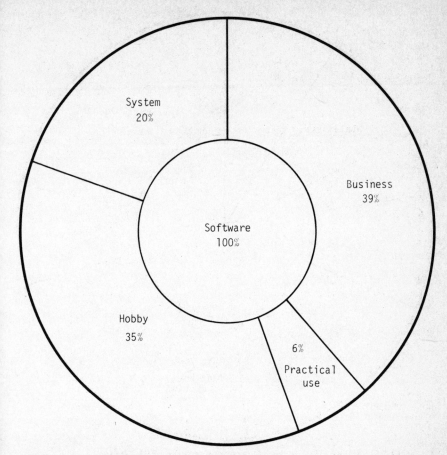

Figure 11   Breakdown of software for 'PC–8000 Series'.

Retailers

The growth rate of personal computer retailers

The number of personal computer retailers is growing by 63 per cent per year, and there are now about 500 stores in Japan. These are mainly specialist computer shops or chain stores, but other types of retailers are also entering the market which is worth $1.5 billion.

Electronic appliance retailers: Akihabara district in Tokyo

This district contains about 200 shops selling many types of electronic appliances and telecommunications equipment. About thirty of the shops have started selling personal computers, and one has had a turnover of nearly $500000 per annum.

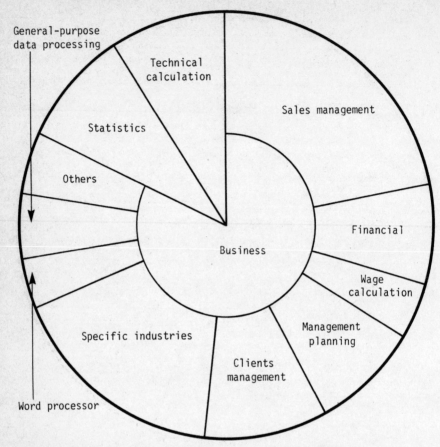

Figure 12   Breakdown of usage for business-purpose software packages.

Department stores

Department stores have also started selling personal computers, competing with office equipment retailers, software houses, and consultants. Chain stores are also beginning to be established.

Department stores are also competing in other areas, providing such facilities as lecture courses on personal computers, advice on which models suit which applications, and developing software and maintenance services.

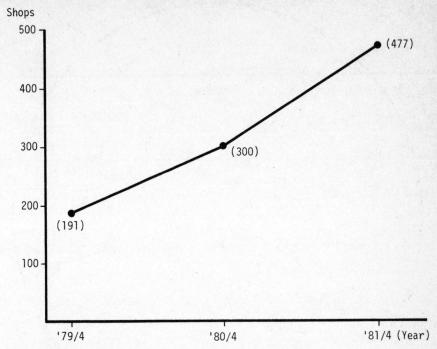

Figure 13   Rate of increase of microcomputer retailers in Japan.

Education

Number of students learning electrical and electronic engineering, and computing

Figure 15 shows the number of students in the various educational establishments studying these subjects. The demand for these graduates exceeds supply, and therefore private education has started to set up personal computer courses. But computer courses are not yet a compulsory part of teaching in Japan and no computer-aided instruction has yet been introduced.

Personal computer schools

There are about thirty secretarial and special schools providing one to two years of computer training, and there are also ten institutions offering six- and twelve-month personal computer correspondence courses. Classes or courses lasting from a few days to two or three months have also become popular. Those offering these courses vary widely and include manufacturers, retail stores, consulting firms, personal computer clubs, the community education divisions of local

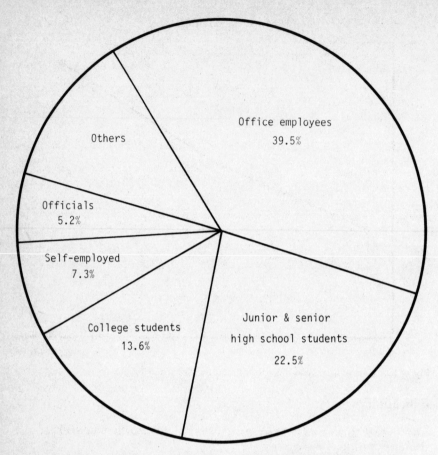

Figure 14   Visitors to the Keio Department Store 1981 microcomputer fair.

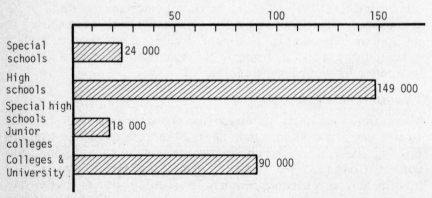

Figure 15   Numbers of students majoring in electrical and electronic engineering, and information processing.

government, computer industry management groups, publishing companies, and privately run education centres. Almost seventy organizations are running such courses, and in the past most of the participants have been hobbyists. The number of businessmen now attending these courses has risen dramatically, and there are also courses available only to women.

In-house training

The larger companies that are promoting office automation have begun to provide organized in-house computer education. Since the personal computer industry is today's most promising market for jobs, public vocational training institutes have also started computer training courses.

Journalism

There are about thirty magazines published each month in Japan on personal computers or microcomputers. They are divided into three categories: hobbyist; technical; and business. Total estimated circulation is about one million—300000 for the hobbyist, 400000 for the technical reader, and 300000 for the businessman. This year other magazines have also published special feature articles on personal computers and office automation, and more than a hundred books have also been published on these two subjects. Book shops are also selling computer instruction manuals which come with cassette-based programs, and two broadcasters have started TV programmes featuring lecture courses on microcomputers.

TRENDS IN TYPES OF USERS

Hobbyists

Microcomputer clubs and their members

There are about 100 microcomputer clubs in Japan and, among their 30000 members, for every seven people there are three students. One per cent of the members are women. Figure 16 shows the breakdown of membership of Japan's largest club, the Nippon Microcomputer Club, which has 7000 members.

The activities of microcomputer clubs

The main activities are exchanging information via the periodicals circulated within a club, inventing and developing hardware and software, and holding seminars on computers.

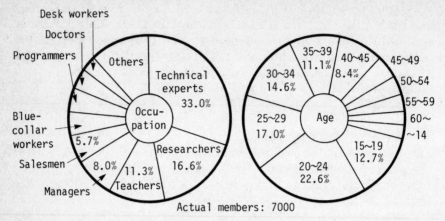

Figure 16   Composition of Japanese Microcomputer Club membership.

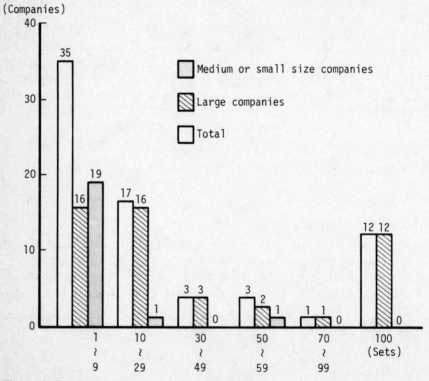

Figure 17   Distribution of personal computers in offices.

Users in industry

The introduction of personal computers into industry

The low price of personal computers has enabled medium, small and even very small companies to buy them, but companies with more than ten personal computers are mainly large firms using them for office work at the departmental level.

Very small companies and offices

Consultants, accounts offices and hospitals have begun to use personal computers rather than employ more staff, and recently very small shops and offices have also introduced them instead of taking on extra workers.

Medium and large companies

In these, microcomputers have been introduced to automate office work, to serve as terminals for general purpose computers, to make graphic plans, and to plan management tactics.

Okamura, an office furniture manufacturer, has a fully automated office as its headquarters, in which general purpose computers link factories to the office. All the documentation used in the headquarters is kept on microfilm, and it is a truly paperless office. The facsimile system is used for inter-office communication, and personal computers are used for office automation, and also as peripheral terminals.

Analysis of personal computer use within a typical company

In administration, personal computers are mainly used to work out statistics, and for office and sales management. In production, they are used as automatic control systems and for technical calculations on planning and development.

General purpose data processing: a tabulation and calculation package

Tabulation and calculation are fundamental elements of administrative work and in the USA one of the best selling software packages for these tasks is Visicalc. The Japanese equivalent of this is called Pips. This is designed to add figures vertically or horizontally and calculate totals and mean values. Techniques for doing such tasks have been vastly simplified, and this software is also suitable for sorting and monitoring, as well as for creating graphics displays.

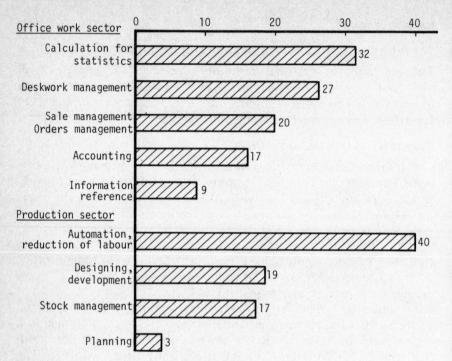

Figure 18 Personal computer usage in companies.

Graphics

Computer aided design is being used to the full in minicomputers. Our institute's GLISP software is used on our own machines. After inputting the coordinates of any three dimensional object, views of that object from any angle can be displayed. More than 1000 different shades of colour are available, although this does depend on the particular hardware used.

Japanese language processing

The Japanese language has three types of script: Katakana, Hiragana, and Kanji. The Roman alphabet is, however, also used as a phonetic system. The Japanese are accustomed to using Katakana to express one syllable and Kanji to express an ideogram, and many have not yet got used to using the Roman alphabet. For them it has been a problem to display Kanji in the form of letters on the computer screen. But a Japanese language word processor has recently been developed that can be interfaced to Japanese-made computers. Some personal computers also include such a word process to make Kanji output possible.

Users in education and welfare

Computer aided instruction in education and welfare is still in the experimental stage, but there has been considerable research into it in recent years. Several types of machines for the disabled have been produced, but high prices have prevented many people from buying them for private use.

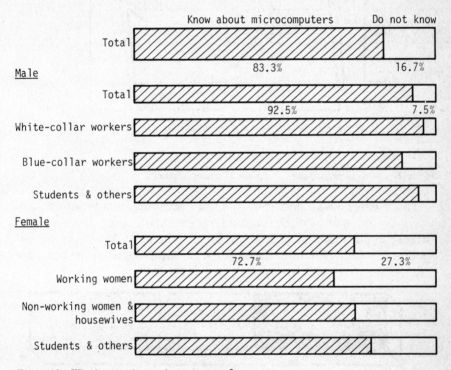

Figure 19   Who knows about microcomputers?

The Japanese public and microcomputers

Figures 19 and 20 show the results of a survey by a private broadcasting company (TBS). The survey sample was about 400 people living in the Tokyo area. The first chart shows how much people know about personal computers. More than 80 per cent have heard of or seen them (making personal computers as well known as ordinary goods). More than 90 per cent of men know of personal computers, and white-collar workers and students know more than people in other categories. Among working women, the percentage is lower than average.

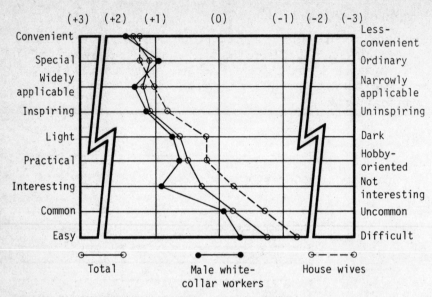

Figure 20   What is the popular conception of microcomputers?

The figures also show how people assess microcomputers. The majority of white-collar workers see computers as 'convenient', 'widely applicable', 'inspiring' machines, whereas housewives are not so enthusiastic. Opinions differ on how much computers can contribute to society and help people live easier lives.

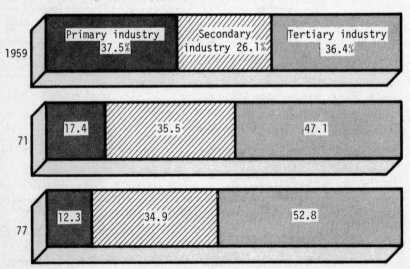

Figure 21   Distribution of workforce by industry category.

THE FUTURE OUTLOOK FOR MICROCOMPUTERS IN JAPAN

It has already been observed that the Japanese have adapted themselves to the computer-oriented society. The reasons for this are found in the various basic elements of Japanese society.

Firstly, Japan is a country with few resources. Secondly, it is a densely populated, highly competitive society. Thirdly, it has a relatively high standard of education. Over a period of more than a hundred years, the social structure of Japan has changed dramatically and each change has been accompanied by technological innovations. For example, after World War II the composition of the work force was transformed. In twenty years or less the number of workers in the primary industries declined rapidly and the number in the tertiary industries grew. The latter seemed to invigorate the secondary industries, causing them to produce more goods for export. Meanwhile, the Japanese economy has been built on a fairly fragile foundation from which to defend itself against international economic fluctuations. Japanese society itself contains various contradictions, and it is important to look at the ways in which the information industry will affect Japan in the future.

The impact of the microcomputer revolution on the social structure

Urban problems

A sizeable portion of the population has been drifting towards large urban areas such as Tokyo and Osaka. Figure 22 shows the discrepancy between the daytime and night-time populations in Tokyo. If this gap was calculated in terms of energy usage, it would be even greater. People drift towards Tokyo in search of the large amount of 'information' available there. When telecommunications and other electronic systems are developed enough to diffuse information easily to remote areas, this centralization of people in urban areas will no longer be a problem.

Energy problems

Microcomputers can contribute significantly towards energy saving by being fitted to equipment that uses large amounts of energy.

Trends in the occupational structure

When telecommunications and electronics are sufficiently advanced to enable people to work at home, employment opportunities for women, old people, and disabled people will increase. Japan has

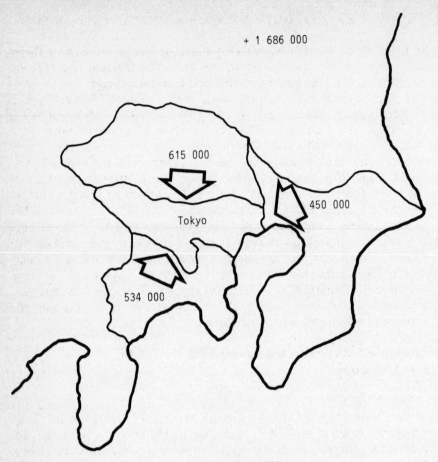

Figure 22 Increase of daytime population in Tokyo (1975).

been rapidly becoming a society with a large proportion of old people, however, and the development of microcomputers will solve some of the problems peculiar to this situation.

The advent of new communications media

More and more of the contents of published material are presented in graphs and illustrations. Further transformations in publishing are possible via the introduction of, for example, personal computers and video discs. If the two are introduced and linked together, the mass media, including publishing and broadcasting, will be affected to an enormous extent.

Information distribution systems that only handle one medium, for example bookstores that sell only books, will collapse, and record

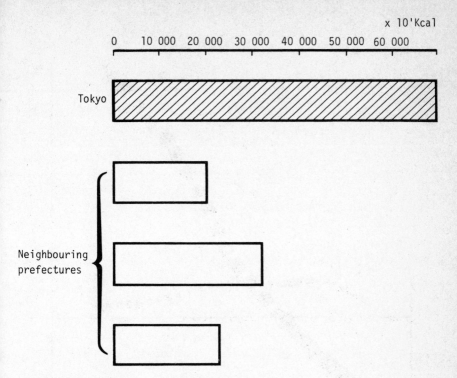

Figure 23 Domestic energy consumption levels.

shops and electronic appliance stores will participate in a new form of information distribution. My institute has recently been developing software systems for the Yokohama Children's Science Museum. In one of the systems now being developed, a question and answer format is used with a combination of keyboard and CRT screen, thus enabling children to learn from the screen. Such a system will naturally change current educational and medical systems.

The importance of software

The social changes caused by transformations in information systems will lead to further changes, but the speed at which this happens will depend on the supply of software. By 1985, there will be 600 000 information processing experts in Japan, but this will not be enough to cope with the rapidly increasing demand for software. According to Boehm, the ratio between hardware and software will become 2:8. This prediction includes only medium and large scale computers, but the same is true of personal computers. So far the development

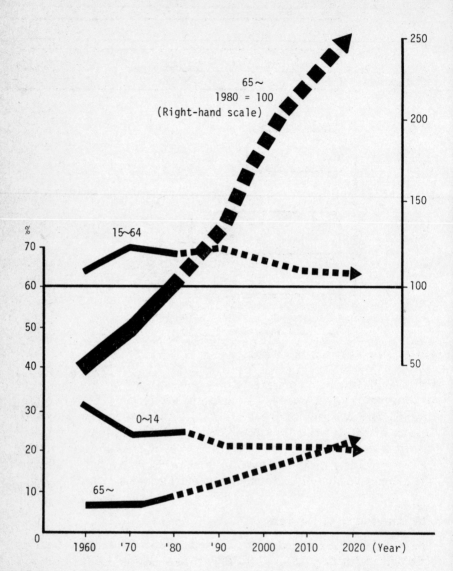

Figure 24   Age distribution trends in the Japanese population.

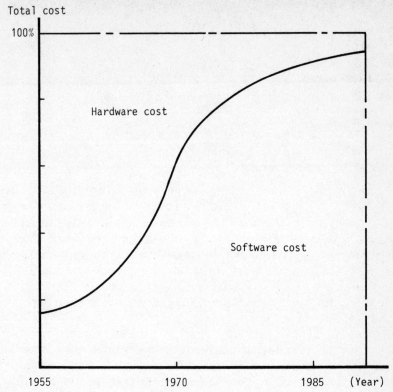

Figure 25 Hardware and software cost shares. *Source*: B. W. Boehm.

of hardware has taken place, but that cannot continue. In the future, software development should assume primary importance, with hardware secondary. To create enough software experts, and to give software development priority over hardware, will require international cooperation in the future.

MICK McLEAN
Editor, Electronics Times, *UK*

One conclusion concerning employment has emerged clearly from the contributors, but to explain it I must first digress for a moment. The debate in Britain about the impact of microelectronics on employment immediately identified two different effects. The first was what you might call the *direct* effect: that as microelectronics technology is introduced into products and processes it has a direct effect on the quantity of labour required in the manufacturing process, on the nature of the products themselves and on the nature of the work involved.

The second effect is *indirect*, which means simply that microelectronics adds a new dimension to international competitiveness. These indirect effects on employment occur when some countries adopt the new technology at a faster rate than others and this in turn has an impact on the competitiveness of the products and consequently on patterns of international trade and employment. The point that has emerged from our contributors is that this second competitive effect is, at least at present, completely dominating the direct effect.

Statistics seem to indicate that countries whose productivity increased fastest have the highest level of employment. In other words, at least in the short term, we are forced, when discussing employment, to include questions of international competitiveness and trade. These are the important issues which need to be tackled now. Perhaps in the longer term, however, the direct effect might predominate.

This brings me to my second theme: that one cannot discuss questions of levels of employment without tackling the question of international competitiveness, and, more specifically, the problem of Japan.

In 1981 Japan was heading for a $23 billion trade surplus with the rest of the world. It would appear that nothing in the future development of Japanese technology will do anything to reverse this trend.

If anything the work the Japanese are doing on office automation, on flexible manufacturing and on mechatronics, can only exacerbate this trend, and worsen an already problematic and apparently permanent trade surplus with the rest of the world.

EMILIO FONTELA
President of the European Association of
Applied Economics

The first point I should like to raise concerns the question of the durability or length of product life. We have been claiming ever since the Club of Rome reports first started prompting concern about the global shortage of materials that the lifetime of products would have to be lengthened. My question to the microelectronics industry would be: how far is the industry going to contribute to such a change in product durability and what would this imply for changes in the structure of production, and employment? It is reasonable to suppose that a move towards more product durability means a shift from employment in production to employment in servicing and maintenance.

My second point concerns the problem of structural integration. Some people understand this to imply the creation of a corporate giant—some degree of integration of companies. I myself understand it in a different way. My understanding is that a number of companies are likely to develop greater interaction among themselves, such as joint ventures and joint facilities for product development. Thus the electronics sector will be more functionally integrated, not necessarily through greater corporate integration, and that in Japan this will take the form of joint ventures between giants in different fields: in consumer products, electronics, machinery, etc.

If I am correct in this interpretation, what it actually means is that the Japanese think that an integrated system of industries will develop around microelectronics technology.

My first question to the Japanese themselves would be to ask about the place of competition within this system. I will attempt to give a partial answer. I have a feeling that this system will evolve a new form of competition. This will consist of competition between the rival strategies of the large groups, so that competition will take place at the level of investment decisions, and the profitability of those decisions, and not at the level of the market.

Some companies will opt for lines of production which are very good, and so they will fare better than other companies, but the market will not be the place where the price war will take place, at least in Japan. From this follows the question: how do these integrated systems work outside Japan? My prospective answer is that they will work like a single company. If I am correct and we see an integrated system working like a single company on export markets, then we can ask: where are the other systems to compete with the Japanese system? Are we in Europe able to build up such a system, or are we going to have a few companies producing one product here and one product there? In that case, obviously, the question of international trade looms large, and we come back to the problem of competition. But my question goes perhaps a bit further and also raises the question of technology transfer. We all agree in Technova that there is an interesting future for technology transfer, in particular between Europe and Japan. But if Japan develops an integrated system, what form can technology transfer take? What can the Japanese then transfer as they obviously cannot transfer the whole system?

In this context we must speak of 'world products'. Just as in the automobile industry we now have the 'world car', maybe in microelectronics we may also have some world products that can be manufactured in different places and still form part of the Japanese system.

SABURO OKITA
Former Minister of Foreign Affairs, Japan
and Advisor to the Japanese Economic
Research Centre

In the world economy Japan has moved into the production of technologically sophisticated products and has started to export these products. We have also gradually moved into somewhat creative areas of technology. I recently asked Mr Ibuka of Sony whether Japanese technology was predominantly imitative or creative. Mr Ibuka replied that the dividing line today between basic and applied research was becoming very obscure. Many Japanese companies are doing what is described as applied research, but their activities are actually very close to basic, fundamental research. Sometimes we hear that Japan concentrates on the commercial application of science and technology and does not contribute enough to the pool of basic scientific knowledge.

Ten years ago I was in Paris as a member of an eight-man study group at the OECD which produced science policy recommendations for the 1970s. The chairman of the study group told me that Japan was drawing on the basic pool of scientific knowledge and using this 'free good' of basic scientific knowledge for commercial applications. Japan, he argued, was earning foreign exchange by exporting the products derived from the international pool of science and technology and the Japanese taxpayer should spend more to fund basic research which would contribute to the common pool of the world's scientific knowledge. That was the story I heard ten years ago at the OECD.

It may be true that our industries have expended more effort in the practical application of theories than in the development of new theories; but as I have said, the dividing line between theory and practice is becoming more and more unclear.

One of the main motivations for Japanese companies to perform research and development, or even invest in risky areas, is the very keen competition that exists between Japanese enterprises. Firms such as Toshiba, NEC, Matsushita, Fujitsu, and many other companies are competing fiercely with each other, and this is somewhat different from the popular image of the Japanese economy, which has been called 'Japan Incorporated'. This image may give the idea that government and industry cooperate very closely and that industry follows government directions with the result that the country as a whole becomes very advanced in technology. I feel this may be a false picture of technological progress in Japan. Keichi Oshima would, I hope, agree that the most crucial factor for technological progress in Japan is the competition between established companies and new entrants to the same markets.

We sometimes say that there is a Japanese custom in Japanese business: that if one company succeeds in a certain area, another ten companies will immediately jump on the bandwagon. The result is a very rapid decrease in the price of the product. The price of some integrated circuits has come down by a factor of ten in a single year. Thus competition between enterprises in Japan is one of the crucial elements for advancement of technology. It leads to a higher level of investment in research and development and a rapid increase in competitiveness in many products. Sometimes companies do not even measure the risk involved in new investments, but go ahead simply because other companies have already done so.

Returning to the question of international competitiveness, we must consider the general adjustment mechanism of exchange rates which is often forgotten. At present the exchange rate is $1 to around ¥230. If the rate appreciates so that $1 is worth ¥200, this will increase the price of Japanese products by over 10 per cent; such a change is perfectly feasible since at the beginning of 1981 this was the actual rate. Yet when the yen weakens on the exchange market, it creates an impetus for Japanese industry to export more, and thus confronts us with a fundamental economic dilemma.

We are competitive because of the price stability of our products; increases in productivity improve our balance of payments and tend to strengthen the yen, probably to even less than ¥200 to the dollar. Yet many of our industries should be able to maintain their competitiveness, at least in electronic products. Automobile exports may diminish somewhat, but Japanese cars will still have some margin, particularly in the US market. So sometimes we must take into consideration the macroeconomic exchange rate as well as the overall picture of the economy when we speak of Japan's role in international trade.

This year (1981) Japan is likely to have a trade surplus of over $20 billion, it is true, but we have a deficit of over $10 million in our invisible trade account, and in 1980 our total current account showed a $6 billion deficit, and a $4 billion deficit the year before that. This year we may thus have a net $10 billion surplus, but this fluctuates from year to year. We need to export to finance our imports of raw materials, energy, foodstuffs and other things.

Some foreign observers accuse Japan of following a policy of mercantilism: just exporting and not importing—but this is plainly untrue. Japan imports many things. We spend, for example, some $60 billion just importing oil, and we have a $30 billion deficit *vis-à-vis* the Middle East which has to be made up by maintaining an export surplus with other areas, otherwise we would not be able to balance our overall trade account.

With likely adjustments in the exchange rate, certain of our products will still be competitive and certain others will gradually lose competitiveness. A very recent case is the aluminium industry, which may disappear in Japan if current economic conditions are maintained. Because of the high cost of energy, Japanese aluminium cannot compete with foreign products. The chemical industry, particularly that producing petrochemical intermediate products, is also becoming less competitive; some of the textile industries, like raw silk and others, are also losing competitiveness to other Asian countries.

We are thus moving into new areas where we can be competitive in order to balance our total trade, including the invisible trade account. Only then will we be able to import oil, food, iron ore and other raw materials, as well as the industrially manufactured products which we cannot produce economically ourselves. This is the way the actual world international economy works.

KEICHI OSHIMA
Department of Nuclear Engineering,
University of Tokyo, Japan

I am an engineer and I have the feeling that engineers do not understand how the exchange rate, or the monetary system, works. This is because it seems that while you are undertaking economic studies, all of a sudden the zero point is dramatically shifted. This, of course, never happens in the case of·physical experiments.

My second point concerns R&D and technology. One view which has been raised argues that if Japan tries to dominate or conquer international markets it will do tremendous damage, not only to Europe and the USA, but also to Japan. This view is certainly true. Nobody in Japan has ever wanted total dominance of the market; we have always wanted a strong Europe and a strong USA. People working in research and development are especially aware of this point because were Japanese products to succeed in dominating totally the markets of other countries the first thing Japanese management would do would be to cut the R&D budget, since in that situation firms only need to maintain product quality. This vision makes engineers such as myself uneasy, because innovation would cease and researchers and engineers would lose their role. I am unable to understand why the economists cannot simply solve the problem of the balance of payments by adjusting the exchange rate, which would let the engineers get on with their work. This may not be an ideal answer, but I would like to have the reactions of a few economists to this point.

KEITH PAVITT
Senior Fellow, Science Policy Research Unit,
University of Sussex, UK

I am not an economist, but I am interested in innovation and want to complement what has been said. I do not want to talk about the implications of industrial activities for the balance of trade, but instead to speak about the international implications of the emergence of a major new area of industrial activity, namely electronics.

There has been a great deal of discussion about the international implications of declining industries, but we have heard far less on the implications for the international political economy of major new industrial activities.

Inevitably innovation, if it is to be stimulated, involves a monopoly element. Somebody must be first and must try to stay ahead.

I would like to draw a historical metaphor between Japan and electronics and what has happened in the past in the chemical industry with regard to the role of Germany. If one looks at the development of the chemical industry it is interesting to note that, like electronics, it was a science-based industry. In fact the first major invention was made not in Germany but in Britain: the development of the first organic dyes in the late 1840s. In the next thirty years a process of massive imitation and then innovation began in Germany. This was based on widespread education, the emergence of large companies, close links between universities and industry and the development of a highly professionalized innovative activity.

This is exactly what one sees today in relation to electronics in Japan. Germany became dominant in the chemical industry, but it was not allowed to maintain that dominance. Other countries bought their way into the industry. They purchased their admission through a combination of protection, industrial restructuring and licensing, and by setting up their own research and development activities. This is the way DuPont emerged behind the American selling price in the USA in the 1920s, and the way ICI developed in Britain. Other countries will not remain passive in response to the geographical spread of major new areas of economic activity; total concentration in one country has never been allowed to happen.

In electronics the same thing is happening. It happened in Europe twenty years ago with the Americans leading the computer industry where governments undertook measures of quasi protection, subsidies and industrial restructuring, in relation to the dominance of IBM and what was then called the 'American challenge'. The same thing is happening today. Dirty games are being played just as historically as they always have been with regard to protection, industrial production and subsidies.

The problem I have, and I think it is an extremely important one, is how does one square this industrial reality in relation to the emergence of a major new area of industrial activity in the industrially advanced countries with the profession of liberalism which is embodied in our international economic system? There are two languages spoken and to some extent there are two realities: what one needs is a means of creating an interface between the two languages so that people can begin to talk to one another sensibly about this sort of question.

LOUIS DE GUIRINGAUD
Former Minister of Foreign Affairs,
France

In closing this examination of microelectronics and daily life, I will try to draw some conclusions. First of all, I have been struck by the extent to which all the contributors underscored the importance of the growth of microelectronics in the electronics industry. This is an aspect that the man in the street will note when he sees small appliances using electronics becoming more and more generally available. In addition, the representatives of the leading firms involved in electronic manufacturing have confirmed that micro-electronics is from now on the branch of their activities which shows the greatest growth and from which they are expecting the brightest future.

At the same time I noted an emphasis on the growing role to be played by the integration of microelectronics, electronic products and software. This integration will come up with consumer products, capable of providing a whole range of services in a convenient manner and these products will be produced by a single supplier whenever possible. These are the technical trends which I think have been identified here.

Another fact which has emerged is the very favourable position that Japan currently enjoys in this new industry. In this respect I agree that when a new industry emerges it is not abnormal for one country to gain a virtually dominant position.

The case of Japan and microelectronics is connected with another point which Keichi Oshima dealt with: the commercial advantage which Japan has acquired in the last twenty years over the USA and Europe. What makes this commercial advantage so unbearable for the USA and Europe is that it is concentrated on industries which involve both a great deal of consumption and also high technology—electronics in particular.

I readily accept Dr. Okita's explanation, since I never thought that the reason for Japan's success was either that it did not spend enough money on basic research or that MITI, whose great power I am acquainted with, was really the concert master for these activities.

The real reason is in fact the ferocious competition that exists between Japanese firms within a single industrial sector. We should not overlook the fact that this fierce competition is what many in Europe vulgarly call savage capitalism. Ferocious competition is something which the Japanese accept and even encourage, but it is no longer very acceptable in Europe or the USA. There is, of course, a certain trend to revise opinions on this, but I doubt that Japanese-style competition will be accepted in societies such as Europe or the USA in the long term.

It has been suggested that there are industries which are going to disappear in Japan and I can readily believe this since the same thing is happening in Europe. Even in the leading industries however—especially electronics—there are also limitations which Japan will encounter. It has been pointed out that when Germany dominated the chemical industry, it ran up against tariff barriers and various other protectionist measures, and hence was not able to retain its dominant position in the long run. History teaches us a lesson which we should learn with care. It indicates that it is only by virtue of cooperative dialogue that fierce competition can be attenuated.

There is a cultural and historical context in Japan which dictates that the Japanese are more active in their work than Americans or Europeans; they are more efficient and they have a more homogeneous market. Therefore it is in the very nature of things that Japan, for the time being, possesses an advantage over Europe and the USA in certain fields such as microelectronics.

Finally, I wish to recall a personal memory of a distinguished Japanese Prime Minister, Mr Fukuda. At the summit meetings of heads of state and government of the industrialized countries in London in May 1977, Mr Fukuda was the head of the Japanese delegation. The French delegation was headed by the President, Giscard d'Estaing; the American delegation was headed by President Carter; Helmut Schmidt represented West Germany and James Callaghan represented the UK.

Mr Fukuda spoke up about economic cooperation. It must be remembered that the heads of state and government were already concerned with the economic crisis. This was a time when we were talking about economic recovery, when we were asking Germany to serve as the locomotive of economic recovery and when we were trying to persuade the Americans to take various measures and Japan was asked to do likewise. Mr Fukuda impressed us greatly, when he said: 'In 1932 I took part in a meeting called by Ramsay MacDonald, the head of the British government at the time, to try to find a solution to the worldwide depression. We were unable to agree. The conference lasted several weeks. Then it broke up and never really resumed. The rest is history, namely the great misfortunes which we all experienced by the end of that very decade, starting in 1940.' So, Mr Fukuda added, 'Let us hope that we are not going to encounter such an unfortunate result once again.'

Since that time, despite the various tensions which we have encountered, the various industrialized countries have been making immense efforts to avoid resorting to the same easy demagogical remedies which some governments could provide: namely protectionism. I hope that our governments will continue to prove that they are responsible and try to avoid protectionist measures. One should nevertheless realize that, for a democratic government which needs to win elections for its very survival, there are moments when it is forced to give voters a certain relief, or satisfaction, by protecting certain industrial activities. This will always be necessary unless we succeed in developing these activities within a framework of harmonious cooperation with those who by virtue of their intelligence, hard work and their history have had the good fortune to become the leaders in a particular industrial field.

I would like to save the last word for the Third World. I chaired the first North–South conference, which started in Paris at the instigation of Giscard d'Estaing in April 1975. The Cancun meeting held in 1981 was an extension of that first Paris conference at an infinitely higher level. I think that on the whole there are reasons for hope and optimism. There is also a great opportunity for Japan and Europe to cooperate with the Third World. I am very close to the opinion of the new French government on the issue of Third World development: the Third World is truly a new frontier which the industrialized nations must try to open up. If we fail to do so, I really do not see how we can manage to emerge from the current economic crisis from which the Third World is also suffering. We must develop cooperation between Europe and Japan with respect to the Third World and we should set this as one of the principal goals for Technova in the future.